Language *for* Learning in the Primary School

Language for Learning in the Primary School is the long awaited second edition of *Language for Learning*, first published in 2004 and winner of the NASEN/TES Book Award for Teaching and Learning in 2005. This handbook has become an indispensable resource, packed full of practical suggestions on how to support 5 to 11-year-old children with speech, language and communication difficulties.

Colour coded throughout for easy referencing, this unique book supports inclusive practice by helping teachers to:

- Identify children with speech, language and communication needs (SLCN)
- Understand speech, language and communication skills
- Consider roles and responsibilities at primary school
- Plan a differentiated and adapted curriculum
- Consider the language demands across subjects
- Adopt a whole school approach
- Make use of a wide range of positive strategies
- Empower children to access the curriculum

Language for Learning in the Primary School comes complete with a wealth of photocopiable resources, giving teachers and teaching assistants the confidence to help children with SLCN more effectively in mainstream settings. It will also be an extremely useful resource for speech and language therapists, specialist teachers and educational psychologists.

Sue Hayden is a speech, language and communication needs trainer with over 30 years' specialist teaching experience both in primary and secondary schools.

Emma Jordan is a service manager and specialist speech and language therapist for the Children's Speech and Language Therapy Service within Worcestershire Health and Care NHS Trust.

Both authors provide training for practitioners working with children and young people of all ages with SLCN and manage the 'Language for Learning' project based in Worcestershire.

nasen is a professional membership association that supports all those who work with or care for children and young people with special and additional educational needs. Members include teachers, teaching assistants, support workers, other educationalists, students and parents.

nasen supports its members through policy documents, journals, its magazine Special!, publications, professional development courses, regional networks and newsletters. Its website contains more current information such as responses to government consultations. **nasen's** published documents are held in very high regard both in the UK and internationally.

Other titles published in association with the National Association for Special Educational Needs (nasen):

Language for Learning in the Secondary School: A practical guide for supporting students with speech, language and communication needs
Sue Hayden and Emma Jordan
2012/pb: 978-0-415-61975-2

Using Playful Practice to Communicate with Special Children
Margaret Corke
2012/pb: 978-0-415-68767-6

The Equality Act for Educational Professionals: A simple guide to disability and inclusion in schools
Geraldine Hills
2012/pb: 978-0-415-68768-3

More Trouble with Maths: A teacher's complete guide to identifying and diagnosing mathematical difficulties
Steve Chinn
2012/pb: 978-0-415-67013-5

Dyslexia and Inclusion: Classroom approaches for assessment, teaching and learning, second edition
Gavin Reid
2012/pb: 978-0-415-60758-2

Provision Mapping: Improving outcomes in primary schools
Anne Massey
2012/pb: 978-0-415-53030-9

Beating Bureaucracy in Special Educational Needs: Helping SENCOs maintain a work/life balance, second edition
Jean Gross
2012/pb 978-0-415-53374-4

Promoting and Delivering School-to-School Support for Special Educational Needs: A practical guide for SENCOs
Rita Cheminais
2013/pb 978-0-415-63370-3

Time to Talk: Implementing outstanding practice in speech, language and communication
Jean Gross
2013/pb: 978-0-415-63334-5

Curricula for Teaching Children and Young People with Severe or Profound and Multiple Learning Difficulties: Practical strategies for educational professionals
Peter Imray and Viv Hinchcliffe
2013/pb: 978-0-415-83847-4

Successfully Managing ADHD: A handbook for SENCOs and teachers
Fintan O'Regan
2014/pb: 978-0-415-59770-8

Brilliant Ideas for Using ICT in the Inclusive Classroom, second edition
Sally McKeown and Angela McGlashon
2015/pb: 978-1-138-80902-4

Boosting Learning in the Primary Classroom: Occupational therapy strategies that really work with pupils
Sheilagh Blyth
2015/pb: 978-1-13-882678-6

Beating Bureaucracy in Special Educational Needs, third edition
Jean Gross
2015/pb: 978-1-138-89171-5

Transforming Reading Skills in the Secondary School: Simple strategies for improving literacy
Pat Guy
2016/pb: 978-1-138-89272-9

Developing Memory Skills in the Primary Classroom: A complete programme for all
Gill Davies
2016/pb: 978-1-138-89262-0

Language for Learning in the Primary School: A practical guide for supporting pupils with language and communication difficulties across the curriculum, second edition
Sue Hayden and Emma Jordan
2015/pb: 978-1-138-89862-2

Understanding and Supporting Pupils with Moderate Learning Difficulties in the Secondary School: A practical guide
Rachael Hayes and Pippa Whittaker
2016/pb: 978-1-138-01910-2

Assessing Children with Specific Learning Difficulties: A teacher's practical guide
Gavin Reid, Gad Elbeheri and John Everatt
2016/pb: 978-0-415-67027-2

Language *for* Learning in the Primary School

A practical guide for supporting pupils with language and communication difficulties across the curriculum

Second edition

Sue Hayden and Emma Jordan

Routledge
Taylor & Francis Group

LONDON AND NEW YORK

Helping Everyone Achieve

First published in 2004 by Language for Learning, Kidderminster

Previous edition published 2007
by Routledge
2 Park Square, Milton Park, Abingdon, Oxon OX14 4RN
In association with the National Association for Special Educational Needs (NASEN)

NASEN is a registered charity no. 1007023

This edition published 2015
by Routledge
2 Park Square, Milton Park, Abingdon, Oxon OX14 4RN

and by Routledge
711 Third Avenue, New York, NY 10017

In association with the National Association for Special Educational Needs (NASEN)

Routledge is an imprint of the Taylor & Francis Group, an informa business

© 2015 Sue Hayden and Emma Jordan

British Library Cataloguing in Publication Data
A catalogue record for this book is available from the British Library

Library of Congress Cataloging-in-Publication Data
A catalog record for this book has been requested

ISBN: 978-1-138-89861-5 (hbk)
ISBN: 978-1-138-89862-2 (pbk)
ISBN: 978-1-315-70821-8 (ebk)

Typeset in Goudy
by FiSH Books Ltd, Enfield
Printed and bound by CPI Group (UK) Ltd, Croydon, CR0 4YY

Contents

Acknowledgements

We would like to thank NASEN for the opportunity to write a second edition of our book *Language for Learning*. We received a great response to the first edition from practitioners working in schools, our colleagues and Language for Learning® trainers. Ten years have passed since our original publication and we still receive positive feedback about how the book offers practical ideas and solutions. *Language for Learning in the Secondary School* was published in 2012 with a simple format and specific guidance on adopting a whole school approach. We have employed the same framework for this edition for primary schools and hope our original readers will find something new to support their work in mainstream classrooms.

Thank you to everyone who promoted and supported the first edition of the book, in particular the Language for Learning® team in Worcestershire – Pamela Connolly, Sheriden Cox and Elaine Packwood. We would also like to thank Phoebe Kent, Teri Rutherford and Jane Smith from our team of Language for Learning® coordinators. Phoebe has supported Language for Learning® for many years both in Dudley and in Worcestershire. Teri and Jane have endeavoured to make a copy of our book available in every school in Kent, making Language for Learning® part of a county-wide approach to supporting children with speech, language and communication needs (SLCN).

Our teams' ongoing commitment to supporting children in mainstream settings is inspirational. We would like to thank Rosalind Pow, Jacqui Woodcock and the speech and language therapists and assistants working in the Children's Speech and Language Therapy Team in the Wyre Forest together with our specialist teacher colleagues in Worcestershire.

Thank you to Language for Learning® for permission to use the illustrations throughout the book. All of the illustrations are by Jacqui Bignell and taken from our Language for Learning® resources and training materials.

Jean Gross enthused all of us during her role as Communication Champion from 2010–11. She truly was a champion for children and young people with speech, language and communication needs, raising awareness and increasing understanding across the workforce. Thank you to Jean for her ongoing support of Language for Learning® and classroom-based interventions.

Finally, thank you to Marie Gascoigne for *The Balanced System®* framework. This framework has shaped our thinking and provided us with a whole workforce solution to meet children's needs. SLCN is everyone's business, we all need to be involved and understand our roles and responsibilities.

We hope this new edition of *Language for Learning* will provide practical, effective support to all practitioners working in mainstream schools.

# Introduction

The original *Language for Learning* book was first published in 2004, winning the NASEN and TES Book Award for Teaching and Learning in 2005. The book proved to be highly popular with practitioners as it offered an easy-to-use format, was quickly accessible and full of practical ideas to support 5 to 11-year-old children experiencing speech, language and communication needs (SLCN). We have worked in partnership for 15 years within the wider *Language for Learning*® project, developing practical training and resources to support practitioners working in mainstream settings. This self-funding, not-for-profit project is jointly owned by Worcestershire County Council and Worcestershire Health and Care NHS Trust supporting a joint, collaborative approach towards meeting SLCN.

Ten years on and much has happened in the field, beginning with the Bercow Report (DCSF 2008) and most recently the publication of the new Special Educational Needs (SEN) Code of Practice (DfE and DoH 2014). During this time much has been written about speech, language and communication needs, commissioning services and evidence-based practice. In the UK we have seen the development of The Communication Trust, a successful national year of communication in 2011, development of the *What Works?* online database of evidenced interventions, a new national curriculum and publication of the Better Communication Research Programme (Lindsay, Dockrell, Law and Roulstone 2012), a landmark extensive programme of interrelated research projects in speech, language and communication needs.

Timeline

Below is a timeline summarising the key events, government initiatives, developments and changes to national policy and practice in relation to SLCN since 2008 in the UK.

2008

Bercow Report (DCSF 2008)

The report included 40 recommendations across a broad range of areas and identified five key issues:

⇨ Communication is crucial
⇨ Early identification and intervention are essential
⇨ A continuum of services designed around the family is needed
⇨ Joint working is critical
⇨ The current system is characterised by high variability and a lack of equity

Better Communication Action Plan (DCSF 2008)

This action plan set out the government's response to the Bercow Report, culminating in the national year of communication in 2011. Some of the initiatives ceased in 2010 following a change of government. The action plan led to:

⇨ The appointment of Jean Gross, the National Communication Champion
⇨ Guidance for commissioning of services following a number of pathfinder projects
⇨ The Better Communication Research Programme
⇨ Hello, the national year of communication

2009–10

Commissioning Pathfinders

Sixteen pathfinder projects were established in 2009 to test ways in which services for children with SLCN could be commissioned effectively. These pathfinders led to the publication of five commissioning tools (Commissioning Support Programme 2011). Guidance and information is provided in relation to each part of the commissioning process including assessing needs, mapping of current provision, workforce planning and evaluating outcomes.

Academies

The Academies Act in 2010 has led to an increasing number of academy schools in England which are directly funded by the DfE and independent of direct control by the local authority.

Academies follow the National Curriculum for core subjects, however, have greater freedom beyond this.

2011

Hello, the national year of communication

Hello aimed to make children's speech, language and communication a priority in homes, early years settings and schools across the country during 2011. Delivered by The Communication Trust, the national year included:

⇨ Publication of information, resources and posters
⇨ A calendar of events such as *No Pens Day Wednesday* and the *Shine a Light Awards*
⇨ Dissemination of best practice

Two Years On: final report of the Communication Champion for children (Gross 2011)

In December 2011 Jean Gross reported on the outcomes from 2010–11. She described the recent progress that had been made, recognised areas of good working practices and made a series of recommendations for government, SLCN bodies and schools. Jean recommended that all schools:

⇨ Understand the impact of poor language and communication skills
⇨ Adopt a three-tiered approach, providing universal, targeted and specialist support
⇨ Commission specialist services to train and support school staff
⇨ Ensure class and subject teachers take responsibility for supporting children with SLCN
⇨ Screen children with behavioural difficulties to identify any underlying language needs

2012

Changes to Ofsted framework (Ofsted 2012)

The Ofsted school inspection framework changed in 2012 to include communication skills; the extent to which:

⇨ Pupils develop their communication skills
⇨ Communication is well taught

Professional Standards for Teachers (DfE 2011)

From 2012, the professional standards for teachers have included an understanding of and responsibility for promoting high standards of articulacy as well as literacy, whatever the subject taught.

Better Communication: Shaping speech, language and communication services for children and young people (Gascoigne 2012)

This publication brought together a sample of good practice identified during 2010–11 and shared at a series of conferences led by Jean Gross and the Royal College of Speech and Language Therapists (RCSLT) in 2011.

The publication includes:

⇨ An introduction to the *Balanced System®* framework and associated tools

⇨ A description of the Worcestershire commissioning project together with other examples of commissioning SLCN services

Better Communication Research Programme (Lindsay *et al.* 2012)

This landmark programme of research was published in December 2012. The report made recommendations within six key areas for:

1. The guidance on the DfE use of the category 'SLCN' in the School Census to be reviewed – the report stated the term was ambiguous leading to confusion within the field
2. Support for developing children's speech, language and communication skills to be conceptualised at three levels – universal, targeted and specialist
3. Services and schools to systematically collect evidence of outcomes that include the perspectives of children, young people and their families
4. A programme of initial and post qualification training, particularly for teachers in changing their classroom practice to support SLCN
5. Health and education to work together to commission and deliver needs-led local services as too many children are still falling through the gaps
6. Consideration to be given to the ways in which research can be integrated to further the development of effective practice

What Works? **database goes live**

The Communication Trust worked with the Better Communication Research Group to develop the *What Works?* database of evidenced interventions, approaches and programmes to support positive outcomes in children's speech, language and communication.

Teachers, speech and language therapists and other practitioners can search the database of interventions by age range, target group, who the intervention is delivered by and the level of evidence available.

2013

The Communication Commitment

The Communication Commitment was launched in October 2013. It is a simple way to develop a whole school approach to communication tailored to the needs of individual schools. Developed by The Communication Trust working in partnership with schools, the Commitment helps to make communication part of school policy and practice to get the best outcomes for pupils.

The Commitment is divided into five areas to help schools address different aspects of communication development. Each area has straightforward and achievable actions to move schools forward. Schools choose an action from each area to create their own Action Plan to take forward and make their Communication Commitment. Practical resources are provided together with signposting to other resources and support to help schools on their journey.

2014

New National Curriculum in England (DfE 2013)

The new national curriculum will be phased in during 2014–15 in primary schools. It calls for the development of pupils' spoken language and vocabulary skills as an integral aspect of the teaching of every subject. Teachers are expected to 'ensure the continual development of pupils' confidence and competence in spoken language and listening skills' (DfE 2013: 15). Vocabulary skills are recognised as key to learning and progress across the whole curriculum.

Special Education Needs (SEN) and Disability Reforms

As part of the wider Children and Families Act 2014, a new Code of Practice for SEN came into force on 1 September 2014. The new Code:

- Emphasises the importance of what can be made ordinarily available at a universal, targeted and specialist level in settings and schools
- Emphasises the role and responsibility of teachers in meeting children's SEN
- Introduces the graduated response – assess, plan, do and review
- Calls for services to be jointly commissioned
- Replaces Statements of SEN with Education, Health and Care Plans

Some of the language we use to talk about speech, language and communication difficulties has changed and the framework we use to plan support for children is different, however, what needs to happen on the ground, in classrooms remains the same. Practitioners need to be confident and competent in identifying children experiencing SLCN as early as possible and providing support at the most appropriate level within the context of the educational curriculum, working in partnership with parents to create a wide range of meaningful language learning opportunities.

The *Balanced System®* (Gascoigne 2012) has shaped our thinking over recent years. It provides a map for services and support for children with SLCN. The system is outcomes focused, describing the elements needed to effectively meet children's needs. It specifies the roles and responsibilities of the wider and specialist workforce; the range of support required at a universal, targeted and specialist level; workforce training and development; and leadership and management of the whole system. Gascoigne (2012) identifies five key strands we need to consider at a universal, targeted and specialist level – supporting **parents and carers**, supporting the **environment** to facilitate communication, supporting **workforce development**, **identification** of SLCN and **intervention** for SLCN. These strands need to be included when planning provision in schools.

This second edition has the same aims as the first, however, the format of the book has been redeveloped, utilising the same framework as *Language for Learning in the Secondary School* (Hayden and Jordan 2012). It provides guidance for some of the strands identified by Gascoigne (2012) including the **identification** of SLCN, supporting the **environment**, working with **parents and carers** and delivery of **interventions** for SLCN at a universal and targeted level in mainstream settings. Specific guidance on adopting a whole school approach and a broader approach to planning within the curriculum, considering each subject area has been included.

The book aims to help readers to:

- Understand speech, language and communication skills
- Identify children with speech, language and communication needs (SLCN)
- Consider roles and responsibilities at primary school
- Consider the language demands across subjects
- Plan a differentiated and adapted curriculum
- Adopt a whole school approach
- Make use of a wide range of positive strategies
- Empower children to access the curriculum

Key to Symbols

Areas of Speech, Language and Communication

Within Chapter 2, areas of speech, language and communication are identified and described. For ease of reference, these areas are both colour and symbol coded throughout the book:

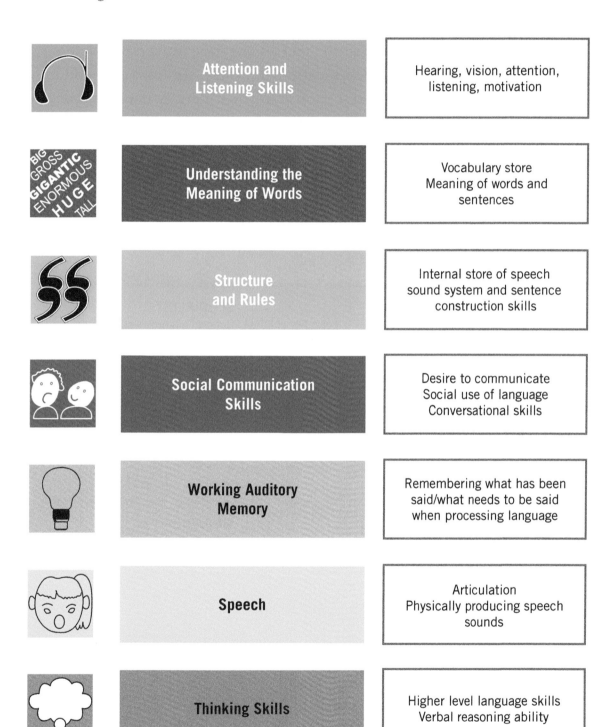

	Attention and Listening Skills	Hearing, vision, attention, listening, motivation
	Understanding the Meaning of Words	Vocabulary store, Meaning of words and sentences
	Structure and Rules	Internal store of speech sound system and sentence construction skills
	Social Communication Skills	Desire to communicate, Social use of language, Conversational skills
	Working Auditory Memory	Remembering what has been said/what needs to be said when processing language
	Speech	Articulation, Physically producing speech sounds
	Thinking Skills	Higher level language skills, Verbal reasoning ability

Levels of Support

Supporting the development of children's speech, language and communication needs at three levels, universal, targeted and specialist, was first introduced to us by Gascoigne (2006) and recommended by the Bercow Report (DCSF 2008) and subsequent Better Communication Research Programme (Lindsay *et al.* 2012). Most recently it can be found in the new SEN Code of Practice (DfE and DoH 2014). Schools need to ensure they are providing support at the most appropriate level, starting with quality first teaching and an effective universal, whole school/whole class approach to identification and intervention. Some children will need some short-term targeted support to further identify needs and develop their speech, language and/or communication skills and a few children will need specialist level assessment and support. The vast majority of children's needs can be met at a universal and targeted level. This book provides an extensive range of strategies and approaches, all of which are identified by level of support:

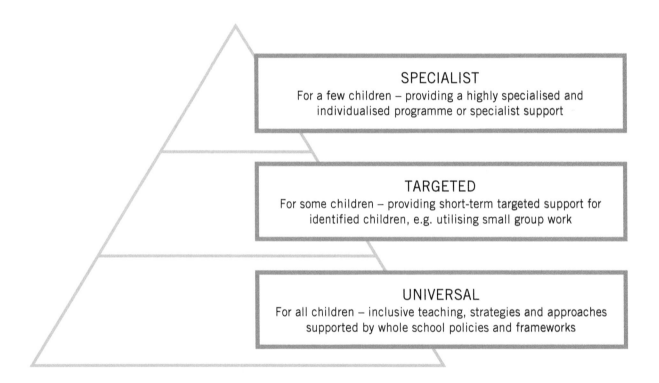

SPECIALIST
For a few children – providing a highly specialised and individualised programme or specialist support

TARGETED
For some children – providing short-term targeted support for identified children, e.g. utilising small group work

UNIVERSAL
For all children – inclusive teaching, strategies and approaches supported by whole school policies and frameworks

Making Practical Use of this book

The structure of the book can be seen below to allow readers ease of access whether considering how to meet the individual needs of a child or planning a whole school approach:

New to SLCN, start here	To develop an understanding of: • Speech, language and communication skills • How language is processed • Receptive and expressive language skills	Go to	**Chapter 2** Speech, Language and Communication Skills
For individual children, start here	To find out how to: • Increase your awareness of speech, language and communication needs (SLCN) within primary schools • Recognise and identify children with SLCN	Go to	**Chapter 3** Identifying Speech, Language and Communication Needs
For a whole school approach, start here	To offer a practical guide to: • Adopting a whole school approach • Understanding roles and responsibilities of primary staff	Go to	**Chapter 4** A Whole School Approach
For curriculum planning, start here	To offer a practical guide to: • Considering the demands and opportunities within the primary curriculum • Taking action to support children with SLCN	Go to	**Chapter 5** Opportunities and Challenges across the Curriculum
For strategies and interventions, start here	For practical suggestions on how to support children with SLCN: • By using positive ways to communicate • Promoting positive, language-friendly environments • Using positive strategies and approaches • Setting up small group targeted interventions	Go to	**Chapter 6** Strategies and Interventions for Use across the Curriculum

The 'graduated response' (DfE and DoH 2014) framework for meeting individual children's needs can be found below:

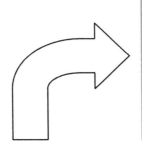

Assess
Go to the Model of Speech, Language and Communication Skills in Chapter 2 and the Identification Tools in Chapter 3, carry out a school-based assessment

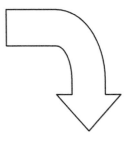

Plan
Consider the demands and opportunities within each curriculum area, plan an adapted or differentiated curriculum using the guidance in Chapter 5

Review
Re-assess and measure progress

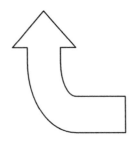

Do
Introduce appropriate strategies and interventions from the suggestions in Chapter 6 and adapt as necessary

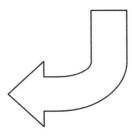

2 Speech, Language and Communication Skills

This chapter describes speech, language and communication skills. It aims to provide practitioners with a shared language to talk about language. It describes the theoretical Language for Learning® model of speech, language and communication skills; identifies and defines areas of speech, language and communication; describes how language is processed and the difference between receptive and expressive language skills.

The Language for Learning® Model of Speech, Language and Communication Skills

The process of understanding and using language is a complicated one, involving a number of different skills. The Language for Learning® model provides a structured approach, a framework for thinking and talking about speech, language and communication skills. Having a shared language to talk about language prevents confusion and can help break down communication barriers created by the use of terminology. Often teaching staff simply do not know where to begin to support a child with SLCN. The model can be used to make sense of observations and assessments, pinpointing specific needs and strengths. As specific areas of language are identified, it is possible to identify areas for development and intervention with confidence. Each area of language is colour and symbol coded allowing all subsequent chapters to give reference to the model.

The Language for Learning® model of speech, language and communication skills can be seen on the following page.

A Model to Represent Speech, Language and Communication Skills

Desire to Communicate
An idea to express and the opportunity to express it

Understanding the Meaning of Words
- Concepts
- Words – vocabulary and word meaning
- Sentences – meaning of whole sentences

BIG
GROSS
GIGANTIC
ENORMOUS
HUGE
TALL

Structure and Rules
- Sound combinations to form words
- Word combinations to form sentences
- Sentences to form narratives

Social Communication Skills
- Conversational skills
- Non-verbal skills – gesture, body language, facial expression, eye contact
- Proximity/distance

Working Auditory Memory
- Remembering what has been said/what needs to be said when processing language

Speech
- Move mouth to form sounds and produce words

Attention and Listening
- Hearing
- Vision
- Attention control
- Motivation

The boxes on the model represent different skills:

Desire to Communicate

This is a fundamental communication skill – the desire to communicate an idea to someone else for either social reasons or to meet a personal need. Children need an idea to communicate, the desire to communicate this idea to another person and the opportunity to do so. This skill is part of 'Social Communication Skills' as described below.

Attention and Listening

This encompasses a range of skills – the ability to hear what has been said; to attend and listen to those involved in the conversation, both the speaker and others listening and being able to sustain this attention for the relevant length of time. It also involves motivation, being interested in what the speaker has to say. In addition to auditory information, children need to be able to attend to the visual information provided, i.e. the non-verbal communication skills being used together with any relevant contextual information. It is also necessary to identify and then eliminate any redundant information, such as extraneous noise or other distractions.

Understanding the Meaning of Words

This is the ability to understand and use vocabulary – words, concepts and sentences. It is a vocabulary store supported by our semantic memory skills. The meaning of the word is stored, e.g. for a concrete object such as a 'bicycle' – what we use it for, where we might find one, the parts it has, the group of words it belongs with and what it looks like. The semantic system is structured and highly organised with words stored by association with other words. Vocabulary development is crucial and 'integral to academic success' (Parsons and Branagan 2014); at age 5 it is one of the best predictors of outcomes for children at GCSE level (Feinstein and Duckworth 2006). As children move through primary school they add to their understanding of vocabulary through exposure within practical, real life experiences and through reading. Knowledge of word meanings is developed over time through repeated exposure across a range of experiences. All new vocabulary introduced within the curriculum relies on this system working effectively.

Structure and Rules

This relates to the set of rules that govern our language system. Literacy development is highly dependent upon these skills. There are three key skills in this area:

- Phonology – the rules that govern how sounds are combined to form words, our speech sound system. In addition to storing the meaning of the word, we also store the sound sequence, so we know that 'car' is made up of two sounds – 'c' and the long vowel 'ar'. Phonological awareness, developed within the foundation stage is the ability to think consciously about these sounds and to use these skills within literacy (Speake 2003). One would expect a child to have both semantic and phonological knowledge of a word, i.e. understand its meaning and its sounds structure (e.g. number of syllables).

- Syntax – the rules governing word order, the way in which we combine words to form sentences and sentences to form longer narratives.

- Morphology – the changes made to the beginnings and endings of words to indicate a change in meaning, for instance adding an 's' to indicate a plural so 'car' becomes 'cars'.

Social Communication Skills

This is the ability to understand and use language in social situations. Skills in this area include conversational skills such as maintaining a topic of conversation, waiting for a turn to speak and non-verbal communication skills such as understanding and use of eye contact, facial expression, proximity and touch. These skills are essential for the development of emotional understanding, social relationships and appropriate social behaviour. Children in primary schools need social communication skills to interact effectively with others, develop friendships, negotiate with their peers and become independent.

Working Auditory Memory

This is the ability to remember information for a sufficient period of time in order to process it and to understand its meaning. It also provides speakers with feedback, keeping track of what has been said and what still needs to be said. Working auditory memory capacity is determined by the end of Key Stage 1 with any future development focusing on strategies to support it.

 Speech

This is the ability to coordinate the mouth to produce the sounds to make words.

Receptive and Expressive Language

There are two ways of entering the model:

Receptive Language Route

In order to understand language, i.e. receptive language, the following route is taken:

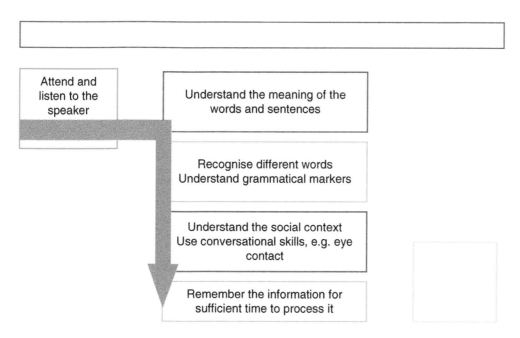

So, receptive language involves all of the language areas. In order to process information and instructions, all areas of language are active and in use.

Expressive Language Route

In order to use language, i.e. expressive language, the following route is taken:

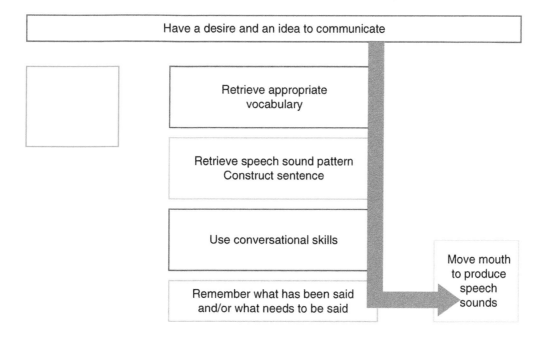

So, using language involves many of the language areas. It is worth noting that the term 'expressive language' is often used to refer specifically to the use of vocabulary and sentence construction skills.

 Thinking Skills

Within Early Years, children develop their ability to use language for social communicative reasons, i.e. to communicate and interact with others. Language and communication skills are developed and used in real life, concrete experiences. The demands and opportunities increase as children start school, language is used **for learning** not just for communicating with the introduction of new vocabulary and social communication rules linked to new social situations and new people. As children move through primary school expectations change as language is used and taught in more abstract and less context-based situations, i.e. talking about objects, events and situations outside of the immediate context. Children need to demonstrate not only the ability to understand and use language in context, but to use **language for thinking**, i.e. verbal reasoning. This involves making use of all of the information available and thinking at an abstract level, considering the language used, the social context, any hidden intent or implied meaning and the thoughts and feelings of others. These skills are needed for children to develop their ability to make inferences, predict what will happen next, give explanations and express ideas, thoughts and feelings.

3 Identifying Speech, Language and Communication Needs

This chapter aims to increase understanding and awareness of speech, language and communication needs (SLCN). It provides information about incidence and a description of the different types of SLCN. To help practitioners recognise children with SLCN, key indicators of difficulties are identified within each of the areas of language introduced in Chapter 2. A guide to school-based assessment, including a range of identification tools is provided. The impact of SLCN on learning and social and emotional development is explored.

Speech, Language and Communication Needs

The ability to communicate is an essential life skill for all young people; it underpins social, emotional and educational development (DCSF 2008). Pupils need to be able to listen, follow instructions, use appropriate vocabulary, construct sentences and use language for social purposes to succeed both academically and socially in school. However, there are many children who struggle to develop these skills. The Better Communication Research Programme recommended a review of the use of the term 'speech, language and communication needs' as it is used inconsistently across health and education, leading to some confusion in the field (Lindsay *et al.* 2012). The term does encompass a wide range of difficulties relating to all aspects of communication (DCSF 2008), so it is useful to consider SLCN within three broad sub-groups (Lindsay, Dockrell, Desforges, Law and Peacey 2010):

1. **Primary** SLCN – where speech, language and communication needs are the child's main difficulty for example a specific language impairment or a specific speech disorder; these difficulties occur in the **absence** of any identified neurodevelopmental or social cause.

2. **Secondary** SLCN – where speech, language or communication difficulties are part of another difficulty or need, for instance a learning, sensory, neurodevelopmental or physical impairment, e.g. SLCN secondary to a hearing impairment, a learning difficulty or autism.

3. **Transient** SLCN – children with SLCN associated with limited experiences, typically associated with but not exclusive to socioeconomic disadvantage. Gross (2013) includes children of 'cash-rich, time-poor' parents starting school with communication difficulties in this group. These difficulties are described as transient; this suggests that given the right support, this group of children have the potential to 'catch up'.

How Many Children Experience SLCN?

National prevalence data suggests up to 10% of all children and young people have long term persistent speech, language and communication needs (Lee 2013). This includes children with primary and secondary SLCN:

- About 7% of children and young people experience specific and **primary** speech and language impairments.
- 3% of children and young people experience SLCN in association with another difficulty, i.e. **secondary** SLCN.

In addition approximately 50% of children at school entry (reception year) in the most socioeconomically disadvantaged populations have speech and language skills that are significantly lower than those of other children of the same age.

Undoubtedly the level of need is high. Some primary schools are dealing with large numbers of pupils experiencing speech, language and communication needs for a range of reasons. A whole school, collaborative approach is vital to ensure pupils' needs are met effectively and efficiently in their school setting. Early identification of difficulties can help to prevent secondary difficulties with the development of social, emotional and academic skills.

Initial Identification

Pupils with speech, language and communication needs often present with a range of difficulties in the classroom, for instance:

- Attention and listening difficulties
- Problems remembering instructions
- Difficulties making themselves understood
- Being the last to complete work
- Immature vocabulary development

- Difficulties making friends
- Being non-compliant
- Giving unusual or unexpected responses to questions

The context, i.e. different people and places will also impact upon a pupil's skills. Some pupils may be able to understand and use language skills in one situation but not another. The school environment and the curriculum bring another set of demands – the use of **language for learning** not just communication, new vocabulary, new situations and new people. As a result of this, pupils with speech, language and communication needs can find school and aspects of school life challenging.

Indicators of SLCN

Children with SLCN may present with a range of difficulties. Indicators of SLCN within each area of language can be seen below:

 Attention and Listening Skills

A child may be observed:

- Finding it difficult to attend to the speaker
- Experiencing difficulty sitting still during whole-class teaching
- Not responding to instructions as part of a group or whole class
- Not asking questions, as used to not understanding, so does not question
- Being more able to engage when visual or kinaesthetic learning opportunities are presented
- Not always complying with instructions
- Relying on peers and copying their actions
- Being distracted by redundant information, i.e. extraneous noise
- Experiencing difficulty staying on task
- Requiring simplified instructions in order to understand

Understanding the Meaning of Words

A child may be observed:

- Having difficulty learning new vocabulary
- Experiencing difficulty understanding language – both at single word and sentence level
- Struggling to find the right word – hesitating, using a similar word, using gesture or mime to compensate or creating new words
- Confusing words belonging to the same semantic group, e.g. says 'yacht' for 'ship'; 'clock' for 'watch'
- Experiencing difficulties learning, retaining and then retrieving new vocabulary
- Learning a word in one situation but then experiencing difficulties applying it or generalising its use
- Experiencing difficulties defining words including identifying similarities or differences between word meanings
- Experiencing greater difficulty with more abstract concepts, i.e. time concepts – next week, last term, the day after tomorrow
- Being inflexible with language, e.g. becoming confused with words that have multiple meanings
- Having difficulty reading for meaning

Structure and Rules

A child may be observed:

- Using immature expressive language – missing words from sentences, confusing the word order or using the wrong word endings

- Misunderstanding instructions or questions that contain negatives, pronouns, plurals and tenses.

- Speaking telegrammatically, i.e. using only the key words needed to convey a message

- Struggling to understand complex grammatical structures, such as connectives – and, so, but, to

- Making grammatical errors in written work

- Struggling to sequence ideas and thoughts so has difficulty recalling events in the correct sequence or telling a story in the correct sequence

- Struggling to make themselves understood, with unintelligible speech

- Experiencing difficulty blending sounds

- Substituting or missing sounds from words

- To have poor phonological awareness, i.e. sound knowledge of a word

- Experiencing difficulties learning new words, i.e. storing the sounds for a new word incorrectly, resulting in inaccurate use.

Social Communication Skills

A child may be observed:

- Lacking flexibility in use of language for a range of social functions, i.e. to share information, to comment, to express feelings, to make a suggestion
- Experiencing difficulties with conversational skills, including:
  - Waiting for and taking a turn in a conversation
  - Initiating and then maintaining a topic of conversation appropriately. A child may have a tendency to talk about a favourite topic
  - Repairing a breakdown when there is a misunderstanding
  - Awareness of the listener's knowledge, providing either too much or too little information for the listener to understand
- Finding it difficult to understand and use non-verbal communication skills, including eye contact, facial expressions, posture and proximity. A child may stand too close to others without realising the implications of this
- Speaking too loudly for the situation or using an inappropriate volume, intonation or unusual voice
- Taking the adult's role
- Talking at people rather than to them
- Not understanding hidden meaning or intent, i.e. making a literal interpretation of what has been said. A lack of use of intent or implied meaning results in a child appearing overly honest or 'blunt'. They may find it difficult to understand jokes or sarcasm
- Struggling to adapt and use language in a flexible way across different social situations

Working Auditory Memory

A child may be observed:

- Forgetting instructions easily
- Struggling to follow long and complex instructions despite appearing to listen
- Forgetting stages within an activity
- Forgetting equipment
- Responding to just the beginning or the end of an instruction
- Following instructions, a child may be unable to repeat or recall what needs to be done in the correct order
- Getting lost within an activity or when giving information
- Losing track in a conversation or a discussion. A child may appear to repeat themselves frequently
- Needing a longer time to process language
- Jumping to the wrong conclusions or giving a tangential reply based on only part of the information given
- Being non-compliant
- Becoming easily confused, particularly during fast conversations or discussions
- Lacking organisational skills

Speech

A child may be observed:

- Experiencing difficulties making themselves understood, they may be unintelligible
- Saying multi-syllabic or complex words inaccurately
- Simplifying words
- Experiencing difficulties with intelligibility within connected speech
- Being dysfluent, i.e. may stammer

 Thinking Skills

A child may be observed:

- Experiencing difficulties using language for complex functions, i.e. to predict, to infer and to reason
- Struggling to assimilate all of the necessary information leading to misunderstandings
- Not considering the viewpoint of others
- Lacking organisational skills

Types of SLCN

As discussed earlier within this chapter, children may experience a primary or secondary SLCN. Potential difficulties within a range of different types of SLCN are presented below to support practitioners in identifying specific needs.

Primary SLCN

Delayed Speech and Language Skills (transient)

Substantial numbers of children are entering school with delayed speech and language skills. In areas of socioeconomic disadvantage the numbers are at their highest. In addition, our changing lifestyle has reduced the amount of time we spend communicating with each other face-to-face. Pupils with delayed skills often have immature development in most/all areas of language.

Potential difficulties	Area
Attention and listening Processing auditory information	
Limited exposure to vocabulary Vocabulary development – breadth and understanding of everyday and subject specific vocabulary Understanding abstract concepts	
Understanding and use of grammatical structures, i.e. tenses, plurals, connectives Phonological skills Sequencing of ideas to form a narrative	
Understanding social rules Using language appropriately across different situations Conversational skills, i.e. turn taking Awareness of other people and ability to interact with peers	
Remembering information presented verbally Following complex instructions	
Articulation	

Receptive Language Difficulties

'Receptive language' refers to understanding and processing language. Pupils with receptive language difficulties are often able to mask problems understanding in the classroom by copying their peers, using visual information, familiar routines and non-verbal information. It does not necessarily follow that a child with good expressive skills or use of language has good receptive skills.

Potential difficulties	Area
Attention and listening skills	
Vocabulary development – breadth and understanding of vocabulary Concept development	
Understanding and use of grammatical language Sequencing and organisational skills	
Keeping up in fast conversations Understanding hidden meaning, non-literal or ambiguous language	
Remembering information presented verbally, sequences of instructions Following lengthy or complex instructions despite listening Time taken to process language	
Verbal reasoning Organisational skills Reliance on and/or preference for a routine	

Expressive Language Difficulties

Expressive language difficulties include vocabulary, using language in meaningful sentences and constructing sentences using grammatical knowledge and skills. These difficulties are easier to identify than receptive language difficulties as a pupil's language may appear immature, disorganised, disjointed or difficult to follow.

Potential difficulties	Area
Vocabulary development – breadth and understanding of vocabulary Word retrieval skills Ability to use and define both concrete and abstract vocabulary	
Word order Sequencing ideas, forming narratives Use of grammatical knowledge in spoken and written language	
Verbal reasoning Use of language for complex functions, e.g. predicting, explaining	

Speech Sound Difficulties

Pupils may experience difficulties developing and using speech sounds. This may be because of a difficulty storing sounds within the phonological system or in articulating sounds. Most likely it is linked to speech sound storage rather than articulating the sound. These children are often identified easily as their speech may be difficult to understand, particularly out of context.

Potential difficulties	Area
Phonological awareness skills Speech sound storage for words	
Articulation Intelligibility	

Specific Language Impairment

Some children experience a primary and specific, persistent receptive or expressive language disorder or impairment. This group does not include children who experience SLCN that is secondary to another need, for example a learning difficulty, physical disability, hearing loss or autism. Identification of SLI will require specialist assessment by a speech and language therapist and specialist teacher or educational psychologist.

Potential difficulties	Area
Vocabulary development – breadth and understanding of vocabulary Defining words Identifying similarities and differences in word meanings Applying or generalising vocabulary Concept development Word retrieval skills	
Word order Sequencing ideas, forming narratives Use of grammatical knowledge in spoken and written language	
Understanding and applying social communication rules Using language effectively in conversations	
Verbal reasoning Use of language for complex functions, e.g. predicting, reasoning, explaining	

Secondary SLCN

SLCN are associated with a wide range of other difficulties. A small range of cognitive, sensory and physical difficulties have been identified below to signpost specific difficulties that may arise.

Anxiety

Children experiencing temporary or permanent feelings of anxiety or great emotional trauma may respond in ways that affect their language or communication skills.	
Potential difficulties	**Area**
Selective talking Use of eye contact Avoidance of verbal responses	
Dysfluency	
Thinking in a flexible way Reliance on and/or preference for a routine	

Attachment

Children experiencing attachment difficulties or an attachment disorder find it difficult to connect to others in an appropriate way. They find it difficult to manage their emotions which can lead to a need to be in control. Attachment disorders are a result of young children not consistently connecting with a parent or primary caregiver and therefore not developing a safe and secure attachment bond.

Potential difficulties	Area
Attention control Listening	
Use of appropriate language in social situations Turn taking skills Use of facial expression Use of appropriate proximity/distance	
Understanding cause and effect in social situations Considering the viewpoint of others Assimilating information Reliance on and/or preference for a routine	

Attention Deficit Hyperactivity Disorder

Pupils experiencing ADHD find it difficult to focus and maintain their attention. They are likely to experience difficulties with cause and effect in social situations; understanding social cues and maintaining attention and listening skills within lesson time. They experience difficulties applying rules in social situations.

Potential difficulties	Area
Attention control Focusing on the speaker Listening skills	
Understanding how words are linked by meaning Sorting and classifying skills	
Turn taking skills, waiting for a turn Maintaining a topic of conversation Use of eye contact Recognition of facial expression	
Understanding cause and effect Assimilating information	

Autistic Spectrum Disorder

Pupils with an autistic spectrum disorder, i.e. autism or Asperger's Syndrome experience difficulties with social interaction, social communication and flexibility of thought. All children with autism will experience SLCN.

Potential difficulties	Area
Attention control Listening Filtering information, not becoming distracted by redundant information	
Understanding the meaning of words Use of sophisticated vocabulary without understanding Understanding how words are linked by their meaning Sorting and classifying skills Defining words and descriptive skills Flexibility, i.e. understanding words with multiple meanings Word retrieval skills Reading for meaning	
Use of language for social purposes, i.e. beyond personal needs Turn taking skills Initiating and terminating conversations appropriately Maintaining a topic of conversation Use of eye contact Use of appropriate proximity/distance Understanding non-verbal communication, e.g. gesture Understanding and using non-literal or ambiguous language	
Understanding cause and effect in social situations Considering the viewpoint of others Using language for complex reasons, i.e. to reason, predict Reliance on and/or preference for a routine	

Cerebral Palsy

Children with cerebral palsy may experience associated language and learning difficulties.	
Potential difficulties	**Area**
Attention control Listening skills Ability to follow instructions	
Vocabulary development – breadth and understanding of vocabulary Sorting and classifying skills Concept development	
Use of facial expression Use of eye contact Understanding social rules	
Following lengthy or complex instructions	
Articulation	
Verbal reasoning skills	

Developing a Second Language

A child in full-time education does not usually have a problem acquiring a second language, provided that cognitive skills, hearing, speech and social skills are developing typically. Developing a second language to the level where it is possible to use language for learning is more challenging and develops over a much longer period of time. A pupil new to English will require support in developing language skills. If there is a concern about language development, it may be necessary to request an assessment in the child's first language.

Potential difficulties	Area
Attention control Listening skills Ability to process auditory information	
Breadth of vocabulary development	
Understanding and use of English grammatical structures Awareness of the English speech sound system	
Understanding social rules and cultural differences Use of eye contact Turn taking skills	
Ability to follow instructions	

Hearing Impairment

Indicators of Hearing Loss

Physical	• History of ear infections
	• Frequent coughs and colds
	• Complaints of earache
	• Breathing through mouth
	• Catarrhal
	• Discharge from ears
Behavioural	• Daydreams
	• Tires easily
	• Is listless
	• Is irritable
	• Is withdrawn – may show little interaction
Functional	• Volume of speech noticeably loud/quiet
	• Has unclear speech
	• Uses limited vocabulary
	• Responds slowly to instructions
	• Responds inappropriately
	• Constantly asks for repetition
	• Turns head to locate sound
	• Cannot function in noisy conditions
	• Relies on facial or lip clues
	• Omits some word endings
	• Has weak phonic skills

Sensori-neural Hearing Loss

Between two and three children in every 5,000 experience a sensori-neural hearing loss. The nerve pathways to the brain are permanently affected, causing mild to profound deafness. The introduction of cochlear implants is changing the needs of this group of children, however, both receptive and expressive language skills may be affected by a hearing impairment.

Potential difficulties	Area
Attention skills Processing auditory information	
Vocabulary development – breadth and understanding of everyday and subject specific vocabulary Concept development	
Understanding and use of grammatical structures Phonological awareness skills	
Fine tuning language according to context Understanding social rules Awareness of others Turn taking skills	
Articulation	

Fluctuating Hearing Loss

This can be very common in primary age children, occurring when there is an infection or build-up of wax. Fluctuating hearing loss can be difficult to assess as a child's hearing levels can vary greatly over a short period of time. Glue ear, 'otitis media' is very common in young children.

Potential difficulties	Area
Attention skills Processing auditory information Distracted by background noise	
Discrimination between similar sounds Phonological awareness skills	
Articulation	

Learning Difficulties

Pupils with moderate or severe learning difficulties will experience SLCN across all areas of language.	
Potential difficulties	**Area**
Attention control Listening skills	
Vocabulary development – breadth and understanding of everyday and subject specific vocabulary Understanding abstract concepts Sorting and classifying skills	
Understanding and use of grammatical structures, i.e. tenses, connectives Sequencing of ideas to form a narrative Phonological awareness skills Rhyming and rhythmic skills	
Using language appropriately across different situations Conversational skills, i.e. turn taking Using language for complex functions, i.e. negotiating, evaluating, complimenting others	
Remembering information presented verbally Following lengthy or complex instructions	
Verbal reasoning Organisational skills	

Specific Learning Difficulties (SpLD)

Pupils who have difficulty in acquiring skills in specific areas – literacy, numeracy and organisation – are often articulate and enjoy talking. There can, however, be difficulty with the language of sequencing, auditory discrimination, auditory memory, classifying and organising vocabulary.

Potential difficulties	Area
Sorting and classifying vocabulary Word retrieval skills	
Following instructions that require sequencing skills Auditory discrimination skills Rhyming and rhythmic skills Sound storage for complex multi-syllabic words	
Following lengthy or complex instructions Remembering information given verbally	
Verbal reasoning Organisational skills	

Visual Impairment

Visual difficulties can range from very mild, corrected by glasses to severe impairments. Visual impairment, which could affect other areas of development, may not be detected until written skills are being developed

Potential difficulties	Area
Following instructions supported by non-verbal or visual clues	
Ability to recognise objects and names Understanding how words are linked by their meaning Understanding abstract concepts Sorting and classifying skills Descriptive skills Awareness of gender and the use of pronouns Use of 'this', 'that', 'here' and 'there' Interpretation of verbs Use of visual terms/concepts Use of prepositions and the concept of space	
Rhyming and rhythmic skills	
Interpretation and understanding of gesture Ability to secure the conversational partner's attention Role play and imitation skills	
Recognition of mouth shapes to make sounds	
Verbal reasoning Organisational skills	

41

Impact of SLCN

Communication 'drives learning and attainment' (The Communication Trust 2013). Speech, language and communication needs can impact on a pupil's academic achievement, behaviour, development of social relationships and emotional development.

Academic Achievement

'Good spoken language skills are strong predictors of later academic success… and predicate reading and writing' (Lee 2013: 12). Vocabulary skills at age 5 are a strong predictor of success at GCSE level and beyond (Feinstein and Duckworth 2006).

Children with SLCN are at greater risk of literacy difficulties. In turn these difficulties can impact on a child's general access to the curriculum, exposure to vocabulary and grammatical knowledge, potentially limiting language development further.

Educational outcomes for children and young people with SLCN at School Action Plus and with a statement of special educational needs are considerably lower than for their peers (DCSF 2008):

- 25% of children with SLCN reach the expected levels for their age in English and Maths at age 11. 80% of children achieve the expected level in English – a gap of 55%; the gap in Maths is 46% and in science it is 41%.
- At the end of Key Stage 4, 15% of young people with SLCN achieve 5 GCSE A*–C or equivalent compared to 57% of all young people (National Pupil Database cited in DCSF 2008).

Social, Emotional and Behavioural Difficulties

Children with SLCN are at risk of experiencing social, emotional and behavioural difficulties. Dockrell and Lindsay (2012) identify the main areas of difficulty as the development of successful peer relationships and prosocial behaviour (helping others, being concerned about others' wellbeing and demonstrating empathy) and the risk of developing emotional difficulties. This report provided evidence that primary aged children with SLCN were **not** at high risk of being recategorised as having behavioural, emotional and social difficulties (BESD) following transfer to secondary school as previously thought.

However, children with SLCN, particularly children experiencing social communication and interaction difficulties are at greater risk of difficulties in this area.

Children with BESD may be experiencing undetected language or communication difficulties that cannot be 'seen' as they are able to use expressive language functionally and speak clearly. Gross (2011) recommends schools screen children with behavioural difficulties in order to identify any underlying SLCN.

Children with SLCN may present with the following behaviours:

- A reluctance to engage, preferring to play or work alone
- Being less likely to start a conversation or interaction
- Withdrawing from or avoiding situations that involve interaction with others
- Disruptive behaviour as a result of poor attention and listening skills or difficulties understanding
- Non-compliance or non-responsive behaviour caused by a lack of understanding
- Time wasting caused by a lack of understanding
- Copying inappropriate behaviour of other pupils without understanding the consequences
- Applying social rules and demonstrating appropriate social behaviour
- Signs of anxiety in new situations or at times of change
- Low self esteem
- Being unreliable in giving information verbally, e.g. recalling past events

Children experiencing long term language and communication difficulties are likely to become increasingly aware of their difficulties as they move through primary school, leading to increased vulnerability to emotional and social difficulties.

Identifying SLCN

A joined up, collaborative approach is essential when identifying speech, language or communication needs. The necessity for 'early' identification and action **regardless of age** was highlighted by the Bercow Report (DCSF 2008). As discussed above, a pupil's skills may vary greatly from one situation to another, so it is vital that the team works together to gain a full picture of a pupil's needs.

There is no single assessment tool that can identify speech, language and communication needs. Schools need to adopt a range of methods. This may include a standardised assessment such as Language Link (www.speechlink.co.uk), a universal screening tool for receptive language, together with a range of observation-based assessment tools.

It is important to:

1. Gather any historical information, for instance early history of SLCN, learning or social needs.
2. Observe a pupil across a range of differing situations.
3. Consider speech, language and communication skills, general learning ability, social and emotional development.
4. Consider the impact of the environment and teaching situation on a pupil's skills.
5. Seek the pupil's views where possible.
6. Involve parents.
7. Gather information from all school staff involved.
8. Consider the need for further assessment by involving outside agencies.

Observation

Observation is a powerful tool and forms the basis of all of the identification tools within this chapter. Observing a pupil across a range of contexts can provide a wealth of information about speech, language and communication skills together with the impact of any needs on social interaction and relationships with both peers and adults. Observation can also highlight potential areas of difficulty across the curriculum and any issues linked to the environment or teaching style that may be impacting upon a pupil's ability to access learning and social opportunities.

It is useful to carry out observations in both structured and unstructured situations across different areas of the curriculum, for instance during playtime, PSHE or circle time and during literacy or numeracy.

Often practitioners have invaluable information about a pupil gained through everyday observations. However, this information may not be recorded or shared in a formal way. It is essential to establish a baseline, identify strengths and needs and measure progress.

Tips for Observation

- Remember observation involves the collection of information, making sense of the findings and then drawing some conclusions.

- Observe the environment and consider teaching style as well as the pupil – language friendly environment tools can be found in Chapter 4, pages 78–85. It is important to consider the impact of the environment on the pupil's ability and may change the focus of intervention from the pupil to the environment and the teacher's communication.

- Observe the pupil in situations that *are* and *are not* language friendly.

- Consider the context, observe in a range of different situations:
  - Location, e.g. classroom, playground, hall
  - Structured lessons and less structured times
  - Type of activity, e.g. lesson, free play, discussion, lunch
  - Teaching situation, e.g. whole class, small group or individual
  - Social situations, e.g. lunch times.

- Think about how information will be recorded and observe discreetly:
  - A nudge or prompt sheet with key words just acting as a reminder
  - A specific identification tool
  - Consider confidentiality, objectivity, professionalism and tact.

- Look for strategies the pupil may be using to support their speech, language or communication skills, for instance using peers as a source of information, their ability to ask for information or clarification, their use of any available visual information.

- Work together to achieve a full picture of a pupil's needs:
  - Gather historical information
  - Discuss the information already known
  - Agree where, when and how the observations will take place
  - Identify strengths and needs
  - Ask the pupil for his/her views
  - Involve parents
  - Ask other practitioners in school for their views
  - Agree how information will be shared.

- Moving forward:
  - Share the findings as a team

– Make sense of the findings using the Language for Learning® Model of Speech, Language and Communication skills described in Chapter 2

– Decide what to do next

– Choose appropriate strategies and interventions as suggested in Chapter 6.

Outside Agency Involvement

It may be necessary to involve outside agencies, e.g. speech and language therapists, educational psychologists or specialist teachers at this stage. Outside agencies will be able to help school practitioners to identify:

- SLCN much more specifically, through the use of formalised assessments
- Specific strengths and needs within speech, language or communication
- Hidden receptive language difficulties that may not be apparent through observation
- SLCN in the context of the pupil's other skills and abilities, for instance if SLCN is related to a learning difficulty or a primary, specific SLCN
- Any associated behavioural, social and emotional needs

Observation-Based Identification Tools

The identification tools provided in this chapter have been designed to help practitioners to make sense of their observations by making links to the Language for Learning® Model of Speech, Language and Communication Skills described in Chapter 2. They are designed to be quick and easy to complete and will lead directly to target setting and strategy/intervention planning.

1 The 'Whole Class Observations' tool on pages 48–49 provides practitioners with the opportunity to record information about a number of pupils within the class. As difficulties are observed, the practitioner records pupils' names and can begin to identify pupils of concern. This tool also enables practitioners to group pupils for small group targeted interventions. This tool has been used successfully at the commencement of an academic year and at the end of an academic year to inform teaching staff in the next year group.

2 The 'Quick Observation-Based Assessment: Speech, Language and Communication Skills' tool on pages 50–52 will remind practitioners of

specific areas of language to observe and consider. Practitioners can use existing knowledge of the pupil to answer each question by ticking the yes/no column and adding any additional comments. Ticks in the 'no' column suggest potential areas of difficulty.

3   The 'Observation Record Sheet' on pages 53–54 is an open recording sheet allowing practitioners to record observations over a period of time within each area of language. A profile can be formed by recording strengths and needs within each area. Additional considerations are listed on the second page.

4   The 'Pupil's Views' rating scale on page 55 can be used with older pupils in primary schools to rate their own speech, language and communication skills. Practitioners can differentiate this resource by providing picture prompts for each of the skills, for instance using pictures taken from classroom rules/routines or task management boards. For younger children in primary schools, practitioners could ask for their views using their visual timetable – for example, the practitioner shows the pupil an activity or lesson and asks for a rating. The rating could be as simple as *thumbs up*, *thumbs middle* or *thumbs down*; a *happy* face versus an *unhappy* face or a posting box using *happy* and *unhappy* pictures.

5   The 'Developmental Chart' on pages 56–57 provides information about the approximate age of development of a number of skills – understanding language, use of language, use of speech sounds, attention control, social behaviour and play skills. This can be useful when trying to establish if a pupil is experiencing a general speech and language delay or a specific difficulty.

6   The 'Information from Parents' record sheet on page 58 is a very simple information sheet to gather information from parents regarding their son/daughter's strengths and needs at home. This can be used as a discussion point when meeting parents as part of the assessment process.

1. Whole Class Observations

Language Areas		Observations	Names
 ATTENTION AND LISTENING SKILLS		• Difficulties sitting still during whole class teaching	
		• Focuses attention very briefly	
		• Does not respond when whole class asked to listen	
		• Instructions need to be simplified in order to be understood	
		• Does not comply with instructions	
		• Does not ask for clarification	
		• Difficulties staying on task	
UNDERSTANDING THE MEANING OF WORDS		• Difficulties understanding new vocabulary	
		• Limited use of vocabulary	
		• Word finding difficulties	
		• Difficulties understanding and using abstract concepts	
		• Difficulties responding to question words	
		• Difficulties defining words or making links between words	
		• Problems reading for meaning	
STRUCTURE AND RULES: SYNTAX		• Difficulties constructing sentences	
		• Uses immature sentences	
		• Uses the wrong tense	
		• Uses telegrammatic sentences, i.e. only uses key words	
		• Puts words in the wrong order	
		• Uses the wrong word endings	
		• Misunderstands negatives, pronouns, plurals and/or tenses	

Language Areas		Observations	Names
 STRUCTURE AND RULES: PHONOLOGY	• Unintelligible speech		
	• Difficulties blending sounds		
	• Substitutes or misses sounds from words		
	• Difficulties with phonological awareness activities		
 SOCIAL COMMUNICATION SKILLS	• Difficulties taking turns or using eye contact		
	• Makes irrelevant comments or asks inappropriate questions		
	• Interrupts/changes the topic of conversation rapidly		
	• Uses inappropriate volume, intonation or unusual voice		
	• Laughs at the wrong time, appears cheeky/rude		
	• Tends to talk at people rather than to them		
	• May take the adult role		
	• Difficulties understanding ambiguous language		
 WORKING AUDITORY MEMORY	• Forgets instructions		
	• Repeats him/herself		
	• Gets lost within an activity		
	• Is unable to recall information or instructions		
 SPEECH	• Repeats him/herself		
	• Difficulties producing speech sounds		
	• Speech deteriorates when excited or nervous		
	• Syllables in multisyllabic words are missed out		
 THINKING SKILLS	• Difficulties using language to predict or make inferences		
	• Struggles to put information together to make sense of it		
	• Lacks organisational skills		

2. Quick Observation-based Assessment: Speech, Language and Communication Skills

Name:		Age:		Date:		
Practitioner:		Year Group:		Review Date:		
AREA OF LANGUAGE		**YES**	**NO**	**COMMENTS**		
Attention and Listening Skills						

1. Does the pupil demonstrate appropriate attention and listening skills during
    • Individual work with adult or a peer
    • In small group work
    • Whole class work						

2. Does he/she respond appropriately during:
    • Small group work
    • Whole class situations						

3. Does he/she respond appropriately to:
    • Instructions
    • Questions
    • Stories
    • Discussions/general conversation						

4. Does he/she ask for clarification or seek additional information?						
Understanding the Meaning of Words						
5. Does he/she understand and use a range of vocabulary, i.e. nouns, verbs, adjectives?						
6. Is he/she able to learn and use new vocabulary appropriately?						
7. Is he/she able to learn and use abstract concepts, demonstrating understanding?						
8. Does he/she respond appropriately to questions, e.g. Who? Where? When? How? Why?						
9. Is he/she able to define familiar words?						

AREA OF LANGUAGE	YES	NO	COMMENTS
Structure and Rules: Syntax			
10. Is he/she able to construct sentences using appropriate grammar, e.g. pronouns, tenses and connectives?			
11. Does he/she use the correct word order when constructing sentences?			
12. Is he/she able to sequence and order information, e.g. with a beginning, middle and end?			
13. Does he/she retell a story or an event in the correct order?			
14. Does he/she respond appropriately to instructions and stories?			
Structure and Rules: Phonology			
15. Does he/she demonstrate sound awareness/knowledge of vocabulary?			
16. Is he/she intelligible?			
17. Is he/she substituting sounds persistently, e.g. using 't' for 'k'?			
18. Is he/she experiencing difficulties acquiring phonological awareness skills during phonics and literacy?			
Social Communication Skills			
19. Does the pupil use his/her language skills for a range of reasons, both functional and social, e.g. to greet, to respond, to comment, to suggest, to negotiate?			
20. Is he/she able to initiate and maintain a conversation?			
21. Is he/she able to end a conversation appropriately?			

AREA OF LANGUAGE	YES	NO	COMMENTS
Social Communication Skills			
22. Does he/she stay on topic?			
23. Does he/she take turns in a conversation?			
24. Does he/she demonstrate an understanding and appropriate use of non-verbal communication skills?			
25. Does he/she provide sufficient information for a listener to understand?			
26. Does he/she recognise and then clarify any misunderstandings?			
27. Does he/she give relevant responses?			
28. Does he/she adapt language use according to the situation and conversational partner?			
Working Auditory Memory			
29. Does the pupil remember information presented verbally, i.e. instructions, information, stories?			
30. Is he/she able to relay messages accurately?			
31. Does he/she repeat him/herself when using language, for instance when giving news or telling a story?			
Speech			
32. Is he/she able to speak clearly, producing speech sounds accurately?			
Thinking Skills			
33. Does the pupil use his/her language skills for complex functions, e.g. to reason, predict, make inferences?			
34. Is he/she able to use language to imagine?			
35. Does he/she express feelings in words?			

3. Observation Record Sheet

Pupil:	Age:	Year Group:
Practitioner:		Timescale:
Contexts observed:		

OBSERVATIONS

 Attention and Listening Skills

 Understanding the Meaning of Words

 Structure and Rules: Syntax

 Structure and Rules: Phonology

 Social Communication Skills

 Working Auditory Memory

 Speech

 Thinking Skills

History of speech, language or communication needs:

Preferred learning style:

General learning ability:

Organisational skills:

Self help skills:

Friendships in school:

Strengths:

Feedback/comments from parents:

4. Pupil's Views

Pupil:	Year Group:	Date:

Instructions:

- This rating scale is designed for older children in primary schools
- Show a picture of each skill or read each skill out for the pupil; simplify the language if needed
- Ask for a rating, supported by visual clues

Skills	☹	😐	☺
Listening to instructions			
Listening to stories			
Sitting still on the carpet			
Sitting still at the table			
Understanding what to do in lessons			
Answering questions			
Remembering new words			
Telling someone about something that has happened			
Telling a story			
Joining in when friends are talking			
Working in groups at the table			
Keeping up when people are speaking quickly			
Remembering what to do			
Remembering what to say			
Speaking to my friends			
Speaking to adults in school			
Speaking to my family			

© 2015, *Language for Learning in the Primary School*, S. Hayden and E. Jordan, Routledge.

5. Developmental Chart

Age	Understanding of Language	Use of Language
0 months ↓ 6 months	• Turns towards sounds • Responds to intonation patterns	• Uses voice and/or body movement
12 months	• Understands short phrases when part of a familiar routine	• Babbles • Begins to express a range of first meanings by gesture and vocalisation, e.g. requesting, rejecting, greeting
18 months	• Situational understanding, i.e. understands key words in familiar, concrete situations	• Uses voice to imitate • Uses facial expressions • Uses single words
2 years	• Understands single words consistently, e.g. find your <u>coat</u>	• More recognisable single words • Occasionally puts two words together, e.g. all gone
3 years	• Understands two key word sentences, e.g. put your <u>train</u> in the <u>box</u> • Identifies functions of familiar objects, e.g. what do you drink from? • Begins to understand abstract concepts, e.g. size and colour • Understands prepositions and negatives • Begins to develop the concept of time	• Uses an extended vocabulary of concrete and abstract words • Puts two or three key word sentences together • Starts to use questions • Learns rhymes
4 years	• Understand three key word sentences • Extends understanding of abstract concepts	• Uses four word sentences • Uses 'and' to link ideas • Uses pronouns, e.g. 'I' and regular plurals • Chats to others during play • Begins to take turns
5 years	• Follows simple stories • Shows greater concentration when listening	• Uses negatives, pronouns, prepositions and past tenses in four to five word sentences • Names, predicts and describes objects and situations • Vocabulary of approximately 5,000 words • Retells stories

Speech Sounds	Attention Control	Social Behaviour and Play Skills
	• Very little attention control • Distracted by every visual and auditory stimulus	• Looks towards adult's face

• Uses
  p,b,t,d
  m,n
  w
• Misses ends of words
		• Friendly with strangers, begins to show signs of anxiety if mother out of sight
		• Takes everything to mouth, reaches for things out of sight

		• Enjoys making sounds with rattles/bells • Enjoys giving and receiving objects • Initiates simple games like hiding toys
	• Single channelled attention	• Some understanding of common danger • Engages in make-believe situations • Unable to share, plays in parallel

• Uses:
  p,b,t,d,k,g
  m,n,ng
  f,s
  w,j,h
	• Still single channelled attention
	• With adult help, will stop what he/she is doing, listen or look at something else and then return to original task
		• Beginning to share and engage in integrated play with other children
		• Shows affection and enjoys helping
		• Can invent people and objects in make-believe play
		• Beginning to accept that needs may not be met immediately

• Uses:
  p,b,t,d,k,g
  m,n,ng
  f,v,s,z,sh,ch,j
  w,l,j,h
	• Will attend to speaker without adult help, but possible to continue the task at the same time as listening	• More independent and strong willed
		• Often quarrels with adults and other children, but is beginning to realise that this should be verbal and not physical
		• Can share and take turns
		• Shows concerns for others

• Uses:
  p,b,t,d,k,g
  m,n,ng
  f,v,s,z,sh,ch,j
  w,l,j,h,r
	• Two channelled attention – can listen and do at the same time
	• Short attention span, but can be taught in small groups
		• Developing 'theory of mind'
		• Plays well with peers both imaginatively and structurally
		• Understands the need for rules and fair play
		• Has definite sense of humour
		• Looks after younger children and animals

6. Information from Parents

Pupil:	Year Group:	Date:
Parent's name and contact details:		

Please comment on:

Your son/daughter's communication skills at home:

Your son/daughter's ability to understand at home, e.g. following instructions, understanding stories:

Social skills:

Your son/daughter's favourite activities:

Any speech, language or communication difficulties experienced in the past:

A Whole School Approach

Providing effective support to develop children's speech, language and communication skills begins at a universal level, it involves the whole school. All members of the school team have a role to play so that pupils have maximum opportunities to learn and generalise skills across school contexts and at home. Everyone needs to be involved to ensure consistency and progression. Working as a whole school team also fosters sharing knowledge of skills, avoiding duplication.

In 2013, The Communication Trust launched 'The Communication Commitment' (The Communication Trust 2013), an online platform to support schools in making a start at adopting a whole school approach. Gascoigne (2012) suggests that a whole school approach should consist of five key strands – supporting parents and carers, supporting the environment to facilitate communication, supporting workforce development, identification of SLCN and intervention for SLCN.

With these five strands in mind this chapter suggests ways in which members of the school team can play a part. The school team will include: leaders (the school's senior management team), the SEN governor, the special education needs coordinator, class teachers, teaching assistants (TAs), administrative staff, lunchtime supervisors (LTSs) and of course, pupils and parents. It will also include the wider workforce in schools and the specialist workforce.

The 'Roles and Responsibilities' tables that follow identify the wider team member's role and links it to Good Practice, Skills and Knowledge, Roles, Strategies and Resources. It also suggests relevant information and materials, some of which are included in this book, others are readily obtainable through the DfE and national organisations.

KEY TO COLOUR CODING
Senior Management Team
Special Educational Needs Co-ordinator
Parents
Pupils
Class Teachers
Teaching Assistants
Lunchtime Supervisors
Administration Assistants
Special Educational Needs Governor
Specialist Workforce

For 'The Communication Trust' resources listed in the tables below please visit their website at www.thecommunicationtrust.org.uk

'The Communication Commitment' can be found at www.thecommunicationtrust.org.uk/commitment

Roles and Responsibilities: Leaders

Good Practice	Skills and Knowledge	Roles and Strategies	Resources
Enhance the social and learning opportunities for pupils with SLCN with awareness and universal strategy training for the school's workforce	Familiar with current national initiatives and research Good understanding of SLCN Knowing the school population and SLCN within the school Understanding the link between SLCN and the specific environmental and social factors of the school's catchment area Awareness of the link between SLCN and behavioural, emotional and social development Knowing that SLCN inclusive provision enhances the learning of most pupils	Work with your SENCO to encourage a whole school approach, sign up to national associations and prioritise training to enhance your SENCO's knowledge and skills Liaise with outside agencies, e.g. the Speech and Language Therapy Service, the Specialist Teacher Service and Educational Psychology	Resources from 'The Communication Commitment' Inclusion Development Programme (DfE)
Whole school audit of SLCN	Adopt a method of: a. identifying the SLCN knowledge and skills of school staff b. identifying the SLCN of pupils c. measuring outcomes	Oversee and interpret audit and outcome measures working with SENCO	*Speech Language and Communication Framework (The Communication Trust)* audit of competencies Identification Tools pp. 46–58 'Language Friendly Environment Tools' pp. 78–85
Development of a whole school approach	Understanding that the challenges facing pupils with SLCN can be supported by creating a Language Friendly Environment	Work with all school staff to implement strategies, as part of a whole school policy Build in teamwork, consistency and progression	'Language Friendly Environment Tools' pp. 78–85

Roles and Responsibilities: SENCOs

Good Practice	Skills and Knowledge	Roles and Strategies	Resources
Speech, language and communication needs awareness training for all staff	Understanding of SLCN Awareness of potential issues for pupils with SLCN Familiar with the SLCF Good training skills	Work with all staff to encourage a whole school approach regarding identification, strategies and resources Support newly qualified teachers	Resources from 'The Communication Commitment' Inclusion Development Programme (DfE) Let's Talk About It – The Communication Trust
Whole school audit of SLCN	Ability to identify need (staff and pupils), plan provision and measure outcomes	Manage information recorded by teachers, TAs and parents	Identification Tools pp. 46–58
Knowledge of universal strategies	Knowledge of general strategies and resources for use at universal level	Build in consistency – use universal strategies throughout the school	Chapter 6 pp. 115–175
Development of a 'Language Friendly Environment'	An understanding of the challenges facing pupils with SLCN and how the school environment has an impact	Implement as part of whole school policy. Provide guidelines for non-teaching staff	'Language Friendly Environment Tools' pp. 78–85
Provision of targeted and specialist interventions	Knowledge of a range of targeted interventions and specialist strategies and resources	Oversee a rolling programme of targeted interventions supporting a range of speech, language and communication skills Discuss and demonstrate specific strategies	Published targeted intervention programmes – What Works? (The Communication Trust) Demonstration pack of resources
TA lesson knowledge	Managing curriculum information	Work with teachers to ensure that TAs know lesson content in advance	'Language Friendly Environment Tools' pp. 78–85

Area	Knowledge/Skills	Action	Reference
Developing pupil independence	Encouraging pupils to develop an ability to take responsibility for their learning	Teach pupils how to use strategies independently	'Developing Independence' p. 87
Good links between school and home	An ability to include parents as part of the school's support team	Gather information and examples to discuss strategies and resources	'Home–School Liaison Checklist' p. 85
Good transition between primary and secondary	An understanding of the challenges facing pupils with SLCN during periods of transition Knowledge of successful strategies	Take time to liaise between schools and develop information packs	AFASIC (The Communication Trust)
Good transition from year to year		Be consistent, pass on identification sheets and continue to use strategies	'Consistency across the School' p. 86
Development of subject-specific strategies and resources	An understanding of how resources can be adapted to make them curriculum friendly. Knowledge of the opportunities and challenges in a range of subject areas	Set up working parties to produce curriculum friendly materials to share	'Introducing Strategies and Resources' p. 116 'Adapting Resources' p. 87
Reinforcement of universal strategies at lunch and break times	Knowledge of the issues facing pupils with SLCN during break times	Train Lunchtime supervisors to use social skills strategies Provide materials	Chapter 6 Social Communication Skills pp. 154–162

Roles and Responsibilities: Parents

Good Practice	Skills and Knowledge	Roles and Strategies	Resources
SLCN training	Desire to know more about your child's SLCN The wealth of knowledge you already have about SLCN	Accept training on offer in school Investigate training opportunities within your authority Go to national organisations online	*School/Specialist Services Handouts* *(The Communication Trust)* National organisations such as NAPLIC, AFASIC and NASEN
Awareness of all strategies being used with your child in school	A willingness to become involved with support in school	Discuss strategies with your child's SENCO, teacher or TA Offer to reinforce at home Accept resources supplied by school to help	School handouts and resources linked to intervention programmes
General support at home to develop useful skills	The belief that it is possible to make a difference	Introduce your son/daughter to the vocabulary of forthcoming topics	Use the 'At Home' strategy sheets to support your child's skills development from Chapter 6
Good home–school liaison	Confidence to share your knowledge and understanding of your child's needs and any effective support strategies Have a consistent approach to communication with school	Seek opportunities to meet with school staff to share information	'Home-School Link Book' (Chapter 6 p. 124) 'Home-School Liaison Checklist' p. 85
Aiding transition from primary to secondary and from year to year	Sharing what you know about your child with secondary school staff Weighing up the school's reputation for SLCN with other factors such as distance from home, friendship groups, out of school activities	Take opportunities to visit your chosen secondary school during years 5 and 6 (social situations are good) Find out what is different about the next year and prepare your child in advance	Use the school's transition pack and consider the suggestions in the Transition Checklist pp. 76–77 to prepare your child for his/her new school

Roles and Responsibilities: Pupils

Information for school staff and parents to discuss with pupils informally and in a way that they can understand

Good Practice	Skills and Knowledge	Roles and Strategies	Resources
Awareness of one's own strengths and weaknesses	An awareness of his/her skills Knowing that most children are good at some things and not so good at others	Think about what is easy and what is difficult in different situations in school Talk to a parent, friend, teacher or TA	
Learning helpful strategies	A willingness to try out and work at strategies that may help with learning and making friends	Have a go at using strategies suggested by teachers, TAs and parents Accept that this may take a bit of hard work to start with and may not go exactly to plan but could be GREAT in the long run Talk to trusted adults about friendship issues	
Using strategies in a variety of situations	Accepting that strategies learned to support the ability to do something may be useful in a lot of other situations	Discuss favourite strategies with the TA or teacher and together adapting them for situations out of school Get family members involved	
Learning to take control	Wanting to do things independently A willingness to work on organisational skills A desire to develop listening skills Being able to take responsibility for not understanding	Use favourite strategies to do things independently Ask for help when understanding is difficult, there is uncertainty or something cannot be found	
Aiding transition from primary to secondary and from year to year	Being curious about what the secondary school will be like Wanting to be prepared	Visit the secondary school during years 5 and 6 possibly for social events Take photos of areas in the school to make it familiar Try to meet other pupils who live nearby beforehand Ask other pupils what will be different	School's transition pack to include the Transition checklist on pp. 76–77

65

Roles and Responsibilities: Teachers

Good Practice	Skills and Knowledge	Roles and Strategies	Resources
Speech, language and communication needs (SLCN) awareness training	Understanding of SLCN Aware of potential issues for pupils with SLCN Familiar with the Speech, Language and Communication Framework Understanding the link between SLCN and behavioural, emotional and social development Remembering that inclusive SLCN provision enhances the learning of most pupils	Take training opportunities Adapt and monitor your communication skills Take responsibility for putting theory into practice Support newly qualified teachers	*Speech Language and Communication Framework (The Communication Trust)* and *'Don't Get Me Wrong' (The Communication Trust)* Inclusion Development Programme (DfE) 'Language Friendly Environment Tools' pp. 78–85 Let's Talk About It – The Communication Trust
Whole school audit of SLCN	Ability to identify pupils' needs, plan provision and measure outcomes	Record observations of pupils' SLCN Share data with other staff	Identification Tools pp. 46–58
Development of a 'Language Friendly Environment'	Knowledge of a range of universal strategies and resources An understanding of the challenges facing pupils with SLCN in primary school	Consider your role in the development of your pupil's speech, language and communication skills and their ability to access the learning environment	Identification Tools pp. 46–58
Working in partnership with teaching assistants	An understanding of the challenges facing teaching assistants Knowledge of the specific needs of the pupils they work with	Support TAs by reinforcing strategies within the classroom and providing lesson plans and vocabulary lists in advance of topics Arrange time to plan together and discuss pupils' need	Liaison sheets Lesson plans Vocabulary lists Opportunities and challenges Chapter 5 pp. 91–114

Area	Knowledge/skills	Actions	Resources
Development of curriculum-specific strategies and resources	An understanding of how resources can be adapted to make them curriculum friendly Knowledge of the opportunities and challenges across the curriculum	Develop resources that are curriculum friendly Work together as a key stage by dividing the work and sharing rather than duplicating Store resources so that they are clearly labelled and easy to access	Chapters 5 and 6
Working with the SENCO and specialist workforce to ensure that interventions are put in place for pupils who require targeted or specialist support	An ability to understand and manage the intervention programme in terms of liaison, making time, possible TA support and feedback	Attend meetings with specialist workforce, parents and SENCO Liaise with parents and TAs explaining intervention, providing resources, supporting and generalising targets in the classroom	Discuss with specialist workforce and SENCO
Developing pupil independence	Encouraging pupils to take responsibility for their learning Supporting teaching assistants when they are encouraging pupils to become independent	Introduce universal strategies such as task management boards with the whole class Take time to teach strategies, adapting to suit the individual and building in consistency and progression Ensure that pupils work towards using strategies independently	'Pupil's Views' rating scale p. 55 'Language Friendly Environment Tools – Pupil's Views' p. 84 'Record of Support' pp. 89–90
Good links between school and home	Accepting that parents know their children well, their view is important and sharing ideas benefits everyone An ability to keep parents included and informed	Discuss and complete the 'Information from Parents' sheet and decide how you are going to work together Provide resources	'Information from Parents' p. 58 'Record of Support' pp. 89–90 See various in Chapter 6 'Home School Link Book' p. 124 and 'Home School Liaison Checklist' p. 85

Roles and Responsibilities: TAs

Good Practice	Skills and Knowledge	Roles and Strategies	Resources
Speech, language and communication needs awareness training	Understanding of SLCN Familiar with the SLCF Awareness of how language skills affect the management and regulation of behaviour and emotions Understanding the link between SLCN and behavioural, emotional and social development	Take training opportunities Take responsibility for putting theory into practice Adapt and monitor your communication skills	Chapters 1, 2 and 3 *Speech, Language and Communication Framework* (*The Communication Trust*) Inclusion Development Programme (DfE) Adult Communication and Classroom Practice' pp. 78–79
Whole school audit of SLCN	Ability to observe pupils and record findings accurately	Record observations of pupils' SLCN, sharing data with teachers and SENCO	Chapter 3 Identification Tools pp 46–58
Development of a 'Language Friendly Environment'	Knowledge of a range of universal strategies and resources An understanding of the challenges facing pupils with SLCN in primary schools Ability to talk to pupils about what is hard and what is easy for them in school	Develop pupils' ability to listen; process instructions and information; understand the meaning of words and sentences; express their thoughts and feelings and make relationships Support their ability to remember what they have to do and what they have been taught	Chapter 5 'Language Friendly Environment Tools' pp. 78–85
Working in partnership with teachers	An understanding of the challenges facing teachers in the classroom An ability to support pupils inclusively	Prepare for lessons in advance, consider vocabulary, visual materials and pupil organisation	Liaison sheets Lesson plans Vocabulary lists

Development of curriculum-specific strategies and resources	An understanding of how resources can be adapted to make them curriculum friendly Supporting a system for storing, sharing and accessing resources	Develop resources that are curriculum friendly, using topic vocabulary Work together sharing ideas and workload rather than duplicating Store for ease of access	Opportunities and Challenges p. 91–114 Adapting Resources p. 87 Chapter 6 – commercial resources (for inspiration) Vocabulary lists
Developing pupil independence	Ability to encourage pupils to take responsibility for their learning Ability to foster independent use of strategies Ability to work with a group of pupils	Take time to teach strategies, adapting to suit the individual and building in consistency and progression Ensure that pupils work towards using strategies independently Check strategy history	'Record of Support' pp. 89–90
Good links between school and home	An ability to keep parents included and informed	Discuss the use of a home-school link book with the SENCO or teacher you work with	Chapter 6 pp. 115–175 Home-school link book p. 124

Roles and Responsibilities: Lunchtime supervisors

Good Practice	Skills and Knowledge	Roles and Strategies	Resources
Basic awareness of speech, language and communication needs	Willingness to attend training by SENCO. An understanding of the link between SLCN and behavioural, emotional and social behaviour	Learn how to communicate with pupils who have SLCN. Understand the challenges they face during the lunch hour. Attend training offered by SENCO	Handouts provided by your SENCO or teacher
Reinforcement of a selection of universal strategies at lunchtime	Ability to use a selection of universal strategies appropriately	Learn to use strategies to help pupils develop their language and communication skills and to reinforce what is being done in the classroom and at home	Active Listening Cue Cards pp. 59–69 'Ideas from Social Communication Skills' pp. 154–163

Roles and Responsibilities: Administrative staff

Good Practice	Skills and Knowledge	Roles and Strategies	Resources
Awareness of the whole school approach to SLCN	Ability to communicate effectively with SLCN pupils	Support pupils with SLCN by following guidelines from SENCO. Be aware of roles and responsibilities of staff, parents and pupils	Guidelines handout provided by your SENCO. Roles and Responsibilities pp. 59–69

Roles and Responsibilities: SEN Governors

Good Practice	Skills and Knowledge	Roles and Strategies	Resources
Awareness of speech, language and communication needs	Willingness to participate in training	Join in with training and supporting theory into practice by helping at a practical level	All chapters Training handouts provided by school SENCO
Awareness of SLCN initiatives prioritised by school leaders and SENCO	Awareness of national guidelines underpinning school initiatives Support school staff with implementation	Discuss initiatives with school leaders and read literature produced by national organisations Offer practical support	Visit The Communication Trust website to see what is available to support the development of speech, language and communication
Awareness of SLCN audit	Understanding why this is important and what the benefits will be	Discuss findings with leaders to support forward planning	School's SLCN audit summary

Roles and Responsibilities: Specialist Workforce

Good Practice	Skills and Knowledge	Roles and Strategies	Resources
Work with other services to establish a common policy to support SLCN in the primary classroom	Having the ability to work with other professionals effectively Sharing knowledge and expertise	Establish regular meetings and working parties with other agencies Share training opportunities Work with other agencies and the school's SENCO on joint projects in schools, e.g. setting up a language friendly environment, staff training	*Identification, Assessment and Intervention* (Hayden and Jordan 2015) Strategies and Resources – Language for Learning Language for Learning Training for Trainers Programme
Ensure that all members of your team receive regular training in identification, assessment, strategies, resources and current initiatives for pupils with SLCN	Familiar with current national initiatives and research Good understanding of SLCN Awareness of the link between SLCN and behavioural, emotional and social development Good knowledge of effective strategies and resources Knowing that SLCN inclusive provision enhances the learning of most pupils	Sign up to national associations, e.g. The Communication Trust, NAPLIC, etc.	*Identification, Assessment and Intervention* (Hayden and Jordan 2015) *Strategies and Resources (The Communication Trust)* Language for Learning KS 1 and 2 Training Programme

Support schools to develop a whole school approach to SLCN incorporating tools for identification, assessment, good practice guidelines and outcome measures	The ability to judge the school's progress in meeting the needs of pupils with SLCN To be able to identify the cooperative and aware members of staff likely to provide leadership	Work with the SENCO to develop a language friendly environment Introduce appropriate methods to identify and assess and measure outcomes for pupils with SLCN	*Identification, Assessment and Intervention* (Hayden and Jordan 2015) *Strategies and Resources (The Communication Trust)* 'Language Friendly Environment Tools' pp. 78–85 'Identification Tools' pp. 46–58
Ensure that all team members are provided with examples of useful strategies and resources for demonstration in schools	Keeping up with current strategies and resources Having the ability to adapt strategies and resources to meet the needs of particular children and settings	Maintain a selection of resources to demonstrate strategies for teachers and TAs Offer informal workshops to discuss the use of strategies and how adaptations can be made Work with other members of your team to extend the resources you have Work on a good storage and lending system in your base	*Identification, Assessment and Intervention* (Hayden and Jordan 2015) *Strategies and Resources (The Communication Trust)* Chapter 5 Education suppliers websites, Appendix 1
Involve parents and carers	Ability to offer encouraging support and reassurance	Explain assessments and interventions Support parents in using strategies at home	*Identification, Assessment and Intervention* (Hayden and Jordan 2015) *Strategies and Resources (The Communication Trust)*

Roles and Responsibilities Tools

The following are all referenced within the preceding roles and responsibilities tables.

1   The 'Transition Checklist for Pupils with SLCN' on pages 76–77 – is a useful list of considerations for parents, primary school staff and secondary school staff.

2   A set of 'Language Friendly Environment Tools' can be found on pages 78–85 and include:

a) Adult communication and classroom practice

b) Providing visual support

c) Creating language learning opportunities in the classroom

d) Managing teaching assistants

e) Developing a skilled workforce

f) Pupil view

g) Home–school liaison checklist

There are many language and communication friendly environmental tools developed by local services and national organisations. The Better Communication Research Programme (BCRP) Communication Support Classroom Observation Tool (Dockrell *et al.* 2012) for Key Stage 1 is evidence based so the tools from our first edition of this book have been brought into line with this so that it is easy for practitioners to use both.

These tools can be used as a checklist by individual teachers monitoring their own practice or as observation record sheets as part of an audit of whole school practice. The 'Pupil View' elicits feedback from individual pupils in relation to language friendly strategies and approaches.

Additional information, considerations and tips can be found as below:

3   'Consistency across the School' on page 86

4   'Adapting Resources' on page 87

5   'Developing Independence' on pages 87–88

6   'Record of Support' on pages 89–90

Transition Checklist for Pupils with SLCN

HOME – How to prepare your son/daughter

Use home visual timetables and set up an evening routine to include homework and getting things ready for the next day	
Practise using plans in shopping malls and town centres	
Organisation: provide a place to work and to keep school clothes and containers to store school equipment, books and work	
Find out about the colour coding used in secondary school and start using it at home to mark books and add to visual timetables	
Discuss the things that your son/daughter will like about their new school	
Practise doing activities in 'lesson length' chunks	
Familiarise your son/daughter with the journey to school	
Discuss issues to do with going to the toilet and illness at school	
Discuss the school rules – what they mean and how they are kept	
Make a pictorial folder for their new school: include information about family and pets, interests, strengths and weaknesses, likes and dislikes, what they are looking forward to and what they are concerned about	

PRIMARY SCHOOL – What to prepare pupils for

Using visual timetables (see p. 121) and homework diaries	
Moving between classrooms	
Working with different teachers during the same day	
Taking responsibility for not understanding	
Asking for and understanding directions	
The names of subjects and other activities in secondary school	
The names of the Head teacher, SENCO, Year 7 teachers and their subjects and TAs (photos if possible)	
Changing for PE quickly	
Make mind maps (see p. 134) of aspects to do with Secondary School	
Make a pictorial folder for their new school: include information about family and pets, interests, strengths and weaknesses, likes and dislikes, what they are looking forward to and what they are concerned about	

SECONDARY SCHOOL – What to provide in advance

Examples of visual timetables (see p. 121) and homework diaries	
Plans of the school with departments, hall, admin and dining areas clearly marked	
Details of the school day: what happens and when, where lockers are, where coats are left etc	
Information about lunchtimes and after school clubs	

SECONDARY SCHOOL – What to provide in school

Buddy system – Year 8 students	
Clear signs around the school – (colour coded if possible)	
Name badges to wear or name labels for desks for both students and staff	
List of school rules to primary school and home	
Colour coded books/subjects and add coding to visual timetables	
Names and photos of key staff – for primary school and home	

PUPIL PROFILE – What to consider

SLCN – Overview of information from any of the 'Language for Learning Identification Tools' (see pp. 46–58)	
Learning style	
Literacy ability	
Emotional literacy	
Flexibility	
Ability to make friends	
Interests	
Health issues and personal hygiene	
Understanding of rules	
Coping with unstructured time	
Response to praise	

DEVELOPING A LANGUAGE FRIENDLY ENVIRONMENT

a. Adult Communication and Classroom Practice

Practitioner: Date:

Skills	In Use	To Develop	Review
Uses pupils' names to secure attention			
Speaks clearly and slowly and gives pupils time to respond			
Uses eye contact, facial expressions, gestures and simple signing when interacting and giving instructions			
Keeps grammar and vocabulary simple			
Keeps questioning to a minimum – uses commenting and describing to engage with pupil(s) or phrases such as 'tell me about ...'			
Makes the order of action the order of mention, e.g. 'Put your name on your work and then hand it in' rather than, 'Hand your work in after you've put your name on it'			
Identifies new vocabulary and explains it			
Explains idioms and non-literal language			
Introduces and controls a variety of noise levels in the classroom			
Varies teaching style			
Uses objects, pictures and symbols to support spoken language			
Provides the vocabulary for unfamiliar actions, objects and concepts			
Positions pupils so that eye-contact can be maintained (pupil–teacher/pupil–pupil)			
Confirms what pupils say by showing understanding of their comments, enquiries or proposals			

Skills	In Use	To Develop	Review
Extends what pupils say by repeating and adding information or more complex grammar			
Provides choices requiring verbal interaction, e.g. 'Do you want to use crayons or felt pens?'			
Reads out what is written on the white board			
Shows finished examples			
Provides clear instructions for homework including 'what', 'when' and 'how'			
Other(s) observed			
Adult Communication: Universal Strategies (Nos in brackets refer to specific strategies in Chapter 6)			
Active Listening p. 120 (25)			
The Ten-Second Rule p. 118 (11)			
Seeking Clarification p. 120 (27)			
*Communication Pace p. 119 (18)			
*Pausing p. 119 (19)			
*Confirming p. 119 (20)			
*Commenting p. 119 (21)			
*Extending p. 144 (5)			
*Labelling p. 130 (2)			
*Open Questioning p. 147 (21)			
*Scripting p. 145 (11)			
Colour coded Worksheets (for older pupils) p. 173 (11)			
Other(s)			

* In line with the *Better Communication Research Programme: Communication Supporting Classroom Observation Tool*, Dockrell, J.E., Bakopoulou, I., Law, J., Spencer, S. and Lindsay, G. (2012)

DEVELOPING A LANGUAGE FRIENDLY ENVIRONMENT

b. Providing Visual Support

Methods	Evidence	Action to be taken	Achieved
Staff awareness of visual recognition levels of development			
Clear signage around the school			
Visual support at appropriate eye-level			
Text supported by photos, pictures or symbols			
Visual timetables displayed in classrooms and corridors for lessons and out of school clubs			
Classroom strategies supported by appropriate visuals			
Routine cue cards displayed in appropriate places, e.g. 'wash your hands' in toilets			
Task management boards used, when appropriate in all lessons			
Word wall with pictures and words of new topic vocabulary			

DEVELOPING A LANGUAGE FRIENDLY ENVIRONMENT

c. Creating Language Learning Opportunities in the Classroom

Class: Date:

	Practice Established	To Develop	Review
Pupils' work is displayed and labelled appropriately			
Small group work targeting speaking and listening development with an adult facilitator is arranged regularly			
Regular sessions of interactive book reading are available			
Opportunities are created for pupils to engage in structured conversation times with adults			
Opportunities are created for pupils to engage in structured conversation times with peers			
All pupils are encouraged to join in with class discussions			
Objects and pictures are displayed that invite comment and discussion			
An area for privacy/quiet is provided			
Study booths are created			
Learning areas are clearly defined			
Literacy areas are provided			
Book specific areas are available			
The classroom is well lit			
Seating is comfortable			
Resources are labelled with words and pictures			
Resources are available for 'finished times'/ free play etc			
An area for imaginative role play is provided that is appropriate for all ages			

DEVELOPING A LANGUAGE FRIENDLY ENVIRONMENT

d. Managing Teaching Assistants

Does the teacher:	Practice Established	To Develop	Review
Clearly specify the TA's roles and responsibilities			
Share information about pupil(s) need(s) with the TA			
Give positive feedback to the TA			
Encourage and support training opportunities			
Instigate regular joint planning opportunities and supply topic information and vocabulary lists in advance			
Clearly specify the aims of the lesson and expectations of pupil(s') contribution(s)			
Value TA feedback and observations			
Manage TA's time efficiently and effectively, e.g. encouraging teaching pupils 'strategies for life' rather than sitting alongside pupils in lessons helping them throughout Use time creatively to support the use of visual information in the classroom with allocated time for resource development Manage small group targeted intervention for language skills, vocabulary development or social communication skills			

DEVELOPING A LANGUAGE FRIENDLY ENVIRONMENT

e. Developing a Skilled Workforce: SLCN Training Record

Whole School

Individual

Name:

Course Details	SLCN Awareness	Identification Tools	Universal Strategies	Targeted Interventions	Specialist Approaches

DEVELOPING A LANGUAGE FRIENDLY ENVIRONMENT

f. Pupil Views

The teacher:	☹ **Strongly disagree**		☺ **Strongly agree**
	1	**2**	**3**
... speaks clearly and slowly			
... talks and listens to me			
... speaks in sentences that I can understand			
... uses words that I understand			
... explains what new words mean			
... makes sure that we understand how to do things			
... shows us what to do as well as telling us			
... uses objects, photographs and pictures when talking – this helps us to understand			
... reads what is written on the white board			
... reminds us of good listening skills			
... gives us time to think			
... encourages us to ask for help or ask questions when we don't understand			
.... uses easy to understand worksheets			

DEVELOPING A LANGUAGE FRIENDLY ENVIRONMENT

g. Home–school Liaison Checklist

Home–school link book (p. 124)
Information and resources about forthcoming topics for pre-learning vocabulary
Regular meetings
List of names, role and contact details of wider workforce involved
Loan of speaking and listening games linked to language group work
Relevant visual cue cards for discussion and practise, e.g. school routine cue cards (p. 120)
Task management boards to help with getting ready for school etc (p. 121)
Visual timetable of school activities including out of school clubs (p. 121)
Invitations for parents to join in with speaking and listening groups in school

Consistency across the School

In developing a whole school approach it is important that attention is given to consistency and progression throughout the school. To maximise opportunities to learn and generalise skills, strategies must be used in a range of contexts. To avoid confusion for pupils all staff must be consistent in the way they are both introduced and used. There will of course be variations on how they are designed to meet the challenges of specific situations, curriculum topics and to cater for individual pupil's needs. Building in progression is obviously important too – strategies and resources will need to be adapted, increasing expectations and reflecting the pupils' growing ability.

Consider the following:

Around the school

- What type of visual support will be used – photographs, pictures, symbols, colour coding etc?
- How will it be displayed – posters, labels, wall charts, cartoon strips etc?
- What will it address – information about school activities, information about behaviour, information to do with health and safety etc? E.g. After-school clubs and societies; how to listen; stranger danger etc?
- How will consistency and progression be built in from Foundation Stage to the end of Key Stage 2, e.g. large coloured photographs at Foundation Stage, coloured pictures in Year 1 and black and white symbols in Key Stage 2?

Learning tasks

- What type of visual support will be used – photographs, pictures, symbols, colour coding etc?
- Who will be responsible for the 'corporate' design and style?
- How will consistency be achieved whilst meeting individual needs?
- How will developmental progression be ensured?
- How will ideas be shared?
- How will resources be shared and accessed?

Targeted intervention

- How will strategies taught in small targeted interventions, i.e. social communication skills groups be reinforced in the classroom, the wider school and at home?

Adapting Resources

There are many resources on the market to address the needs of young children with SLCN but many of them need adapting in order to target specific skills and/or reduce the time needed to use them.

Consider the following:

- Take inspiration from traditional board and card games often designed for pre-school children
- Make the game short so that it can be played at the end of an activity or lesson – a little and often is the best way to develop skills and reinforce vocabulary
- Use curriculum-specific vocabulary and pictures
- Take advantage of the social opportunities games create – development of skills, e.g. turn-taking, and relationships
- Store for ease of access and opportunity to share. Leave directions with the resource and encourage colleagues to add their adaptations

Developing Independence

Developing independence is a challenge for most pupils but those with SLCN have particular difficulty as, in general, instructions are given verbally rather than through demonstration. Limited time is often available to make these expectations clear or to practise how to achieve them. So for the SLCN pupil, who may lack organisational skills, developing independence can be a challenge. It is important therefore to create opportunities to teach these skills and reinforce them in every context possible.

Consider the following:

- Expectations – how will consistency across the school and progression from year to year be ensured?
- Communication – how will support be given so that school routines are communicated to pupils with SLCN?
- Coping by oneself – how will adults encourage pupils to think and act for themselves?
- How will the school work with parents to ensure some consistency between home and school?

Some useful strategies and resources include:

- School routine cue cards (see p. 120 strategy 28)
- Visual timetables (see p. 121 strategy 29)
- Visual timelines – a strip placed around the form room with main events marked and an arrow pinpointing 'today' (see p. 135 strategy 30)
- Task management boards (see p. 121 strategy 32)
- Labelled resources

Record of Support

Name: Year:

Need	Strategy	Adaptations	Progression
Poor attention and Listening in whole class situations	Active Listening Cue cards taught in class – large cards displayed on wall – CT to remind Date: 23.04.14	Introduced reinforcement with TA in small groups and at home Date: 03.05.14	Occasional reminder in group sessions. Cue cards still used in class. Date: 20.06.14
Poor vocabulary retention	What is it? Poster displayed on classroom wall – use as reminder/ frequent activity for whole class. Small group activity using What is it? Board to reinforce selected vocabulary from topic work Date: 23.04.14	No adaptations necessary Date: 03.05.14	Use What is it? Board as a reminder independently when asked about a word in a small group Date: 20.06.14

Record of Support

Name: _____   **Year:** _____

Need	Strategy	Adaptations	Progression
	Date:	Date:	Date:
	Date:	Date:	Date:

5 Opportunities and Challenges across the Curriculum

Opportunities for developing speaking and listening are found in all areas of the curriculum. The new National Curriculum (DfE 2013) sets out a list of spoken language skills that pupils are expected to have been taught by the end of primary school. These skills are broad and include many sub-skills.

This chapter considers these spoken language skills together with the opportunities within the curriculum for developing them and the challenges facing pupils with SLCN. Curriculum areas which are 'hands on', visual or active offer more opportunities for those with language needs to understand, process and develop the language being used.

Two tables, colour and symbol coded to match the Language for Learning® Model of Speech, Language and Communication Skills (p. 12) and the Language Areas in Chapter 6 are provided to support practitioners in the classroom.

National Curriculum (2014) – Spoken Language Skills Years 1 to 6 (pp. 92–94)

- Identifies the spoken language skills that the new National Curriculum expects pupils to achieve by the end of Year 6
- Links these skills to the areas of language defined in Chapter 1
- Suggests specific strategies to support the development of these skills located in Chapter 6

SLCN opportunities and challenges of each subject area (pp. 95–114)

- Identifies the opportunities and challenges across the curriculum in subject areas
- Suggests some solutions
- Links the opportunities, challenges and solutions to the areas of language identified in Chapters 1 and 6
- Directs practitioners to specific approaches, strategies and activities described in Chapter 6

National Curriculum (2014) – Spoken Language Skills Years 1 to 6

Skills	Area(s) of Language	Strategies and Interventions to Consider Chapter 6
Listens and responds appropriately to adults and their peers		Teach listening skills and appropriate social interaction by selecting strategies and activities from Attention and Listening (pp. 117–129), Social Communication Skills (pp. 154–163) and Memory and Language (pp. 164–168).
Asks relevant questions to extend their understanding and knowledge		Encourage pupils to take responsibility for not understanding by providing a questioning culture in the classroom. Use prompts such as the Seeking Clarification Cue Cards (p. 120 strategy 27). Use Question Cue Cards (p. 172 strategy 3) to reinforce pupils understanding of question words.
Uses relevant strategies to build their vocabulary		Adopt a systematic approach when introducing new vocabulary. Read through Understanding the Meaning of Words (pp. 130–142), select and adapt strategies to make them curriculum friendly, in particular the word association activities.
Articulates and justifies answers, arguments and opinions		Work on sentence structure (p. 145 strategy 13), cause and effect (p. 174 strategy 14) and expressing opinions (p. 174 strategy 16). Increase confidence through discussion in small groups involving simple, personally experienced situations. Use visual support – photographs or pictures and appropriate recording frames for ideas and discussion prompts.
Gives well-structured descriptions, explanations and narratives for different purposes, including for expressing feelings		Work on sentence structure (p. 145 strategy 13) and story-telling (p. 146 strategy 18). Teach visualising skills (p. 174 strategy 18) and how to describe simple objects using a framework such as the What Is It? Board (p. 132 strategy 12) and group activities (p. 158 strategy 26). Use visual prompts such as Feelings Cue Cards (p. 159 strategy 32) to name and discuss feelings.

Maintains attention and participates actively in collaborative conversations, staying on topic and initiating and responding to comments		Teach active listening (p. 120 strategy 25) and select strategies from Attention and Listening (pp. 117–129). Develop turn-taking skills (p. 159 strategy 29). Support topic maintenance using the Talk Time strategy (p. 160 strategy 33). Set up a social communication skills group for those struggling in this area. Work on working auditory memory to develop the ability to process what is being heard and remember what to say – look in Memory and Language (pp. 164–168) for appropriate activities.
Uses spoken language to develop understanding through speculating, hypothesising, imagining and exploring ideas		Teach core vocabulary. Use Recording Frames (p. 173 strategy 9) and a selection of activities from Thinking Skills (pp. 172–175).
Speaks audibly and fluently with an increasing demand of Standard English		Read through Structure and Rules (pp. 143–153) to ascertain which area(s) pupils are struggling with and select suitable strategies and interventions. Prioritise speaking and listening activities to develop skills and increase confidence.
Participates in discussions, presentations, role play/ performances, improvisations and debates	ALL	To participate in a range of high-level speaking and listening activities especially with an audience requires a great deal of confidence. To gain confidence, all areas of speaking and listening will need to be prioritised. Take every opportunity to include an oral element in class activities. Use visual support, situations within the child's experience and a safe environment to practise.
Gains, maintains and monitors the interest of the listener(s)		

Skills	Area(s) of Language	Strategies and Interventions to Consider Chapter 6
Considers and evaluates different viewpoints, attending to and building on contributions of others		Encourage children to consider the views of others and develop their interactive skills. Create a safe environment that is conducive to expressing one's views and listening to others effectively. Look at the range of suggestions in both Social Communication Skills (pp. 154–163) and Thinking Skills (pp. 172–175).
Selects and uses appropriate registers for effective communication		Support pupils who have difficulty interacting with others by setting up Social Skills Groups to work on conversation skills and behaving appropriately in different contexts (p. 158 strategy 28).

ART AND DESIGN

Opportunities and Challenges	Solutions	Language Area	Numbered strategy from Chapter 6
Listening to and processing instructions	Teach listening skills Give pupils processing time Use visual cues		25 Active Listening 11 Ten-second Rule 28 School Routine Cue Cards
Remembering the sequence of what to do and when	Use prompting devices		32 Task Management Boards
Selecting and naming equipment	Label storage spaces and equipment		23 Organise and Label
Understanding new terminology, e.g. words to do with art and craft media such as, charcoal, pastels and collage or words to do with technique such as shading, spraying and sketching and words to do with observation such as perspective, texture and tone	Provide word definition activities to teach nouns e.g. pastel, glue gun Provide visual/kinaesthetic support for more complex vocabulary e.g. charcoal, quilted, collage etc		12 What Is It? Board 15 Interactive Concept Posters
Working with others on joint projects	Be clear about who is doing what Provide opportunities to practise social skills		26 Group Rules Posters 28 Social Skills Groups
Accepting praise and taking criticism	Make comments specific and honest		15 Praise and criticism
Visualising the finished product from a description	Show finished examples Teach visualising skills		4 Examples 18 Visualising

Art & Design provides a positive environment for language challenged pupils as they are able to learn language through 'hands on' experience.

COMPUTING

Opportunities and Challenges	Solutions	Language Area	Numbered strategy from Chapter 6
Listening to and processing instructions	Teach listening skills Use visual support		25 Active Listening 24 Visual Cueing
Remembering the sequence of what to do and when	Use prompting devices		32 Task Management Boards
Understand use of algorithms	This is dependent on pupils having an understanding of a sequence of processes rather like a recipe. Make sure explanations are given with visual support such as simple flow charts		45 Flow diagrams
Recognise uses of IT	Consider all aspects and record as a mind map		25 Mind Maps
Communicate online safely and respectfully	Create a safety rules poster with pupils and refer to it regularly		26 Group Rules Posters
Collect data appropriately	Practise data collection by asking questions and recording through role play (including how to greet and round off)		

COMPUTING

Opportunities and Challenges	Solutions	Language Area	Numbered strategy from Chapter 6
Present data appropriately	Show finished examples, start by asking for one style of presentation, then limit pupils to a choice of two and gradually increase choice		4 Examples 6 Flow Diagrams 7 Venn Diagrams
Use logical reasoning to make predictions Design and write programmes to achieve specific goals, including problem solving	Work on cause and effect across the curriculum always starting with pupils' own experience. Help pupils to identify key information by breaking down into stages and checking understanding of each stage		13 Sorting and classifying 14 Cause and effect 17 Problem solving 16 Expressing opinions

DESIGN AND TECHNOLOGY

Opportunities and Challenges	Solutions	Language Area	Numbered strategy from Chapter 6
Remembering the sequence of what to do when	Provide prompting devices		32 Task Management Boards
Selecting and naming equipment	Label equipment, provide visual diagrams		23 Organise and Label
New terminology for materials and processes	Provide word definition activities to teach nouns		12 What Is It? Board
	Provide visual/kinaesthetic support for more complex vocabulary e.g. photographs/ diagrams and examples		15 Interactive Concept Posters
			25 Mind Maps
	Use visual support		
	Provide subject specific word dictionaries		27 Personal Word Book
			28 Visual Dictionaries
Working on joint projects	Be clear about roles		28 Social Skills Groups
	Provide opportunities to practise social skills		26 Group Rules Posters
	Use social skills posters		
Accepting praise and taking criticism	Make comments specific and honest		15 Praise and criticism
Visualising the finished product from a description	Show finished examples		4 Examples
	Teach visualising skills		18 Visualising
Talking about ideas and comparing finished products	Teach the core vocabulary to talk about the design of the product – see interactive concept poster above		
	Provide a recording template divided into key elements for comparison		9 Recording

Design and Technology provides a positive environment for language challenged pupils as they are able to learn language through 'hands on' experience.

ENGLISH

Opportunities and Challenges	Solutions	Language Area	Numbered strategy from Chapter 6
Listening and responding appropriately	Work on listening skills Speak slowly and clearly Allow processing time		25 Active Listening 18 Pacing 19 Pausing 11 Ten-second Rule
Maintain attention	Use visual support		24 Visual Cueing, Gesture and Mime
Remembering and processing what has been said then formulating a related idea and remembering it until there is a chance to speak	Give pupils time to process, set up small discussion groups		11 Ten Second Rule
Understanding the meaning of words and how they change in different contexts	Plan vocabulary and teach in a structured way Provide personal/class dictionaries		12 What Is It? Board and Word Definition Cue Cards 27 Personal Word Book
Learning words with multiple meanings	Use visual devices		24 Word Webs
Remembering/understanding the plot and the relationships between characters in stories	Present the plot and character relationships visually		25 Mind Maps 45 Flow Diagrams
Understanding character types, situations and scenes	Link new characters/situations and scenes to what pupils already know		
Articulating sounds Remembering, differentiating and blending sounds Segmenting words into syllables Finding words that rhyme Identifying initial sounds	Literacy skills are dependent on the ability to make the sounds to form words; being aware of the sound combination in words; manipulating those sounds to form different words and developing sound knowledge about words		Seek help from your Speech and Language Therapist or Specialist Teacher. Look at Structure and Rules: Phonology pp. 149–152 and select appropriate activities and strategies

Opportunities and Challenges	Solutions	Language Area	Numbered strategy from Chapter 6
Asking appropriate questions	Develop understanding and awareness of different types of questions		20 Question 21 Open Questioning
Early story writing	Discuss sequences Use objects, pictures, prompt cards and planners Work on tense Encourage pupils to extend their sentences by modelling		11 Scripting 13 Sentence Work 14 Narrative Skills 18 Story Planners 23 Plurals 17 Acting out stories 5 Extending
Participating in speaking and listening activities	Role-play situations with pupils practising in more than one role.		38 Role play
Initiating and responding to comments			
Using appropriate register and proximity	Use visual prompts		
Putting oneself in another's place	Provide opportunities to attend social skills groups		26 Group Rules Posters 28 Social Skills Group
Empathising with characters in stories	Link to what the pupil already knows		
Understanding non-literal phrases	Always explain – use commercial resources		What Did You Say – What Do You Mean? – Commercial Resources p. 162
Staying on topic	Be firm and provide visual prompts		33 Talk Time Boards

Opportunities and Challenges	Solutions	Language Area	Numbered strategy from Chapter 6
Visualising characters/scenes/situations from a description or in order to write a description	Show pictures or dramatised clips to accompany prose or to stimulate the imagination Teach visualising skills		18 Visualising
Explaining/discussing ideas Considering and evaluating different viewpoints	Teach the core vocabulary to talk about ideas – see purple logo earlier Use mind mapping or provide a recording form divided into key elements for comparison		10 Mind Maps 9 Recording
Predicting outcomes	Work on cause and effect		14 Cause and effect
Organising information/thoughts Linking ideas and making connections	Use mind mapping and flow charts		10 Mind Maps
Giving structured descriptions/explanations Adult Child	Repeat using a simplified form Provide recording templates		9 Recording

GEOGRAPHY

Opportunities and Challenges	Solutions	Language Area	Numbered strategy from Chapter 6
Listening to and processing instructions	Work on active listening Keep language simple and chunk information		25 Active Listening
Processing and remembering a high volume of new information	Refer to relevant visual cues as you are speaking Try to 'remind' rather than 'test' when recapping		12 Positive Statements 21 Commenting
Learning new vocabulary	Pre-teach vocabulary and provide visual information		23 Pre-teaching
Generalising words/information	Use displays to help pupils remember key words and information		25 Mind Maps
Coping with concepts outside personal experience	Provide word dictionaries		27 Personal Word Books 28 Commercial Visual Dictionaries
Using unfamiliar vehicles of factual representation – maps, atlases, globes and symbols	Visit relevant places to experience some unfamiliar aspects first hand Start by observing and describing something very familiar such as an aerial view of the pupil's table top, recording as a simple diagram Play matching games to reinforce what symbols mean		Google Earth (Commercial Resources) p. 139 35 Snap and Pelmanism

GEOGRAPHY

Opportunities and Challenges	Solutions	Language Area	Numbered strategy from Chapter 6
Working with others on joint projects	Consider the dynamics of the group Be clear about roles Use social rules posters Provide small group support for pupils with social interaction difficulties		26 Group Rules Posters 28 Social Skills Groups
Having the ability to understand that one's environmental circumstances impact on the way one lives	Role play living in different locations, e.g. describe one's day		38 Role Play
Remembering instruction/information long enough to process it and respond	Give pupils time to think about what has been and construct a verbal response		5 Ten Second Rule
Using his/her imagination	Teach visualising techniques		18 Visualising
Ability to extract and organise relevant information	Use mind mapping followed by sequencing main points from the mind maps		10 Mind Maps

HISTORY

Opportunities and Challenges	Solutions	Language Area	Numbered strategy from Chapter 6
Listening to and processing instructions	Teach listening skills and give pupils thinking and response time		25 Active Listening 11 Ten Second Rule
Processing a high volume of new information	Use visual support Keep language simple and chunk information		24 Visual Cueing 1 Speak clearly
Learning new vocabulary	Pre-teach vocabulary – consider both concrete words such as nouns, e.g. queen, gas mask etc and abstract words such as adjectives, e.g. bright, rough etc		12 What is it? Board 24 Word Webs 15 Interactive Concept Poster
Coping with time concepts	Use timelines for decades, centuries etc		4 Time concepts
Generalising words/information Coping with concepts outside personal experience	Provide subject specific dictionaries Visit relevant places to experience some aspects first hand (a quarry/mine) or to set the scene (a castle/an air raid shelter) then record as a poster, a diagram or a flowchart Watch DVDs		27 Personal Word Books 28 Commercial Visual Dictionaries 15 Interactive Concept Poster 45 Flow Diagrams
Understanding that in earlier times people's views and experiences would be quite different from ours	Relate to real life experiences Role-play situations with pupils practising in more than one role to experience other points of view		
Working with others on joint projects	Consider the dynamics of the group Be clear about roles Provide opportunities to practise social skills Use social skills posters		28 Social Skills Groups 26 Group Rules Posters

HISTORY

Opportunities and Challenges	Solutions	Language Area	Numbered strategy from Chapter 6
Remembering instruction/information long enough to process and reply to it	Give pupils time to think about what has been said and formulate a response		5 Ten-Second Rule
Remembering the point to be made whilst waiting for a turn	Regular activities to help develop working auditory memory will strengthen this skill		Memory and Language activities pp. 165–166
Comparing different ways of life and points of view	Use recording frames to list differences; paste pictures or draw if writing skills are weak – always start from what pupils already know		9 Recording frames
Weighing up advantages and disadvantages			
Considering causes of change	Use mind mapping followed by sequencing main points from the mind maps		10 Mind Maps
	Work on cause and effect		14 Cause and effect
Distinguishing between facts and opinion Comparing interpretations of an event	Provide a recording form divided into key elements for comparison		9 Recording frames
Using his/her imagination	Teach visualising techniques		18 Visualising

MATHS

Opportunities and Challenges	Solutions	Language Area	Numbered strategy from Chapter 6
Listening to and processing instructions	Work on listening skills Use visual cues Simplify instructions so pupils understand the sequence of what they have to do		25 Active Listening 28 School Routine Cue Cards 14 Sequence instructions
Selecting equipment and calling it by the correct name	Label storage spaces with pictures/symbols and names of equipment		23 Organise and Label
Learning the order in which to do tasks within a maths activity	Provide visual and tactile prompts		32 Task Management Boards
Discriminating between similar sounding numbers, e.g. sixty and sixteen	When talking about numbers speak clearly, writing any that could be misheard on the white board as you speak Work on auditory discrimination skills		Select from Structure and Rules – Phonology pp. 150–152

MATHS

Opportunities and Challenges	Solutions	Language Area	Numbered strategy from Chapter 6
Learning the basics – days of the week, months of the year, quantity, volume, tables etc	Do not assume retained knowledge of this Refer regularly to information pasted onto maths book/file or displayed on wall	big GROSS GIGANTIC ENORMOUS HUGE TALL	
Understanding time concepts	Provide visual prompts see visual timetables in Attention and Listening p. 121		30 Visual Timelines
Understanding prepositions	Use hand positioning when talking, e.g. in, on, under		
Ability to use common vocabulary for comparison, e.g. heavier and lighter etc	Teach 'lighter' and 'not lighter' first to avoid confusing opposites		
Using words that have different meanings in other contexts, i.e. table, figure	Check understanding of the word – ask pupils what it means Provide visual reminders		24 Word Webs
Understanding maths symbols, e.g £, +, = etc	Match symbol to definition by playing snap and matching games		Maths Concept Wheel – Commercial Resources p. 138
Working in a group on a joint project	Be clear about roles Provide opportunities to practise social skills Use social skills posters		28 Social Skills Groups 26 Group Rules Posters
Understanding question words	Develop understanding and awareness of different types of questions		20 Questions

MATHS

Opportunities and Challenges	Solutions	Language Area	Numbered strategy from Chapter 6
Retaining information long enough to work out what it all means and work out the maths	Provide visual and tactile support Work on working auditory memory Encourage pupils to make notes to increase confidence		22 Task Management Boards 25 Messengers 26 Kim's Game 27 I went to market …
Collecting data	Practise asking questions and recording through role play (including how to greet and round off) see Social Communication Skills p. 158 strategy 28		9 Recording
Extracting relevant information	Provide clear simple sheets for collecting information Use highlighting		11 Colour coded texts
Developing sequencing skills			
Explaining a process/method Linking ideas and making connections	Provide recording frameworks suitable for the task, e.g. flow charts for sequencing and explaining a process or method, mind maps for connecting ideas and Venn diagrams for comparing and contrasting		6 Flow Diagrams 10 Mind Maps 7 Venn Diagrams
Developing flexibility of thinking as maths requires pupils to use a range of skills – switching from one to another during the same activity	Use symbols to prompt which skill to use Teach the rules and point out the logic		8 Symbols

MFL

Opportunities and Challenges	Solutions	Language Area	Numbered strategy from Chapter 6
Listening to and retaining unfamiliar sounds, words and phrases	Use recording devises for pupils to practise sounds/words and to listen to the correct form Adapt ideas from phonological activities		Structure and Rules – Phonology pp. 150–152
Learning new words for vocabulary that is already understood	Reduce the number of words to learn Encourage role play in small groups Provide visual support		
Learning new words for vocabulary that is not understood	Translate word definition strategies into the language being taught This will also practise question phrases		12 What Is It? Board
Pace may be an issue – new vocabulary introduced too quickly to assimilate	Use sales catalogues and flyers in new language for cutting out and sorting		
Working on everyday topics – good opportunity to practice social skills and revisit situations not fully understood	Work in small groups/pairs use ideas from social skills group activities Role-play situations		28 Social Skills Groups
Using unfamiliar speech patterns may be useful for pupils with poor speech as most of the class will be having similar difficulties	Practise sounds as a whole class or in small groups Use songs and raps		

MUSIC

Opportunities and Challenges	Solutions	Language Area	Numbered strategy from Chapter 6
Listening and attending	Teach listening skills		25 Active Listening
Remembering the sequence of what to do when	Provide visual prompts from basic conducting to flow diagrams showing the sequence of the rhythm or the playing order of instruments		32 Task Management Boards
Understanding new terminology	Use subject specific word books/files Recording devices such as talking glossaries		27 Personal Word Book 26 Talking glossaries
Auditory discrimination	Work on auditory discrimination adapting activities to incorporate musical sounds		Select from the range of activities in Structure and Rules: Phonology pp. 150–152
Development of many skills underpinning communication and literacy, i.e. aural perception, rhyming, oral discrimination, patterns of spoken language, memory etc	Take this opportunity to set language to music/raps and chants to help students expand on sentence structure and narrative skills		12 Group speaking and chanting

MUSIC

Opportunities and Challenges	Solutions	Language Area	Numbered strategy from Chapter 6
An ability to compare pieces of music	Work on 'same and different' Start with the sounds musical instruments make – use pictures of instruments to sort into types extend to pictures of images conjured up by various sounds Expand to include rhythm, pitch, mood and feelings	GROSS BIG ENORMOUS GIGANTIC HUGE TALL	
An understanding of different genres and the influences that have created them	Use sorting and classifying activities Adapt Lotto – provide boards with symbols representing each type of music – cover with counters when genre is identified Encourage pupils to discuss music with their parents and grandparents to make a timeline or bar chart of most popular music		39 Sorting and classifying 30 Visual Timelines
The ability to talk about music in relation to emotion	Understand emotive vocabulary		32 Feelings Cue Cards

PHYSICAL EDUCATION

Opportunities and Challenges	Solutions	Language Area	Numbered strategy from Chapter 6
Understanding rules from verbal instructions Listening to instructions whilst engaged in an activity	Pre-teach rules, use diagrams and role play Work on dual attention Break the activity/game down into short sequences with pictures or symbols e.g. for rounders change 'Hit the ball, run towards the first post, look to see how far the ball has gone, decide how far you are running' to 'hit, run and look, decide'		32 Task Management Boards
Getting ready for PE – organisational and sequencing skills	Give very clear directions Work on speed and keeping clothes tidy to save time		28 Routine Cue Cards
Selecting the correct equipment – knowing what it is called	Label equipment and its storage space Provide posters showing which sports equipment is required for which game		23 Organise and label 12 What Is It? Board
Understanding verbs	Demonstrate the action whilst verbalising the word Reinforce using visual prompts Use mime or gesture, e.g. hopping, skipping		Talkabout … things we do Commercial Resources p. 138
Safety issues	You may need to spend more time helping pupils with SLCN to understand safety requirements in PE Do not give too much explanation – use symbols and clear, simple instructions		
Working with others to create a gym or dance sequence	Provide an ideas frame and a flow chart frame Be clear about roles		9 Recording

SCIENCE

Opportunities and Challenges	Solutions	Language Area	Numbered strategy from Chapter 6
Learning the names of specific science equipment	Label storage spaces with pictures/symbols and names of equipment		23 Organise and label
Remembering the sequence of what to do when	Use visual prompts Use visual cues Refer to posters and diagrams		32 Task Management Boards 29 Visual Timetables
Learning new vocabulary	Keep language simple and chunk information Pre-teach vocabulary using prompting activities Provide word dictionaries		23 Pre-teaching 27 Personal Word Book
Identifying and naming plants and animals – i.e. knowing what is the same and what is different e.g. what makes a frog a frog and not a newt Comparing and classifying Describing change	Teach simple word definitions Make use of 'Interactive Posters' Use recording devices to produce talking glossaries Provide activities to reinforce the vocabulary		15 Interactive Concept Posters

SCIENCE

Opportunities and Challenges	Solutions	Language Area	Numbered strategy from Chapter 6
Linking ideas and making connections	Provide recording frameworks suitable for the task, e.g. flowcharts for sequencing and explaining a process or method, mind maps for connecting ideas and Venn diagrams for comparing and contrasting		9 Recording 11 Colour coded texts 6 Flow Diagrams 10 Mind Maps 7 Venn Diagrams
Selecting salient points	Sort key points onto an 'order of importance' chart		
Predicting outcomes			
Solving problems, arriving at conclusions etc	Work on cause and effect		17 Problem solving 14 Cause and effect

Science provides a positive environment for language challenged pupils as they are able to learn language through 'hands on' experience

Strategies and Interventions for Use across the Curriculum

This chapter aims to provide practitioners with a wealth of strategy and activity ideas to support pupils with language and communication needs across all areas of the curriculum.

It is divided into the seven areas of language identified in Chapter 1. Each section is colour- and symbol-coded to match the Language for Learning® model of speech, language and communication skills and lists the observed behaviours for difficulties in each area.

Language development cannot be seen as separate from the delivery of the curriculum. When choosing strategies to meet individual needs, it is important to consider the whole context. Consider how strategies and resources can be used at a universal, whole class level together with small group targeted interventions. Working in this way will be of benefit to other pupils in the classroom and will help to promote the general development of speaking and listening skills. It will also ensure the provision of meaningful, context-based language learning opportunities, supporting generalisation of skills into real life situations. This chapter provides a range of strategy and activity ideas for practitioners to support pupils across the curriculum. The suggestions are a starting point and will need to be adapted to suit the needs of individual pupils and settings. Some strategies appear in more than one section as they address more than one area of language.

The strategy ideas are sub-divided into:

- **Positive communication** – ways practitioners can improve their delivery
- **Universal strategies and approaches** – for inclusive practice for the benefit of all pupils
- **Targeted strategies** and approaches which provide support for those pupils identified as having SLCN

Examples are given of how these strategies can be presented to parents so that development can continue at home.

Introducing Strategies and Resources

Consider the language and communication demands of curriculum topics

(Refer to 'Opportunities and Challenges within the Curriculum' pp. 91–114)

→

Consider the language and communication needs of your pupils

(Use the 'Identification Tools', Chapter 3 pp. 46–58)

→

Select universal and targeted strategies and interventions from Chapter 6

↓

Match responsibilities to school staff

(Decide who will be responsible for what to avoid duplication)

Assess effectiveness

(What can pupils do now they could not do before?)

If successful build in progression

↑

↓

If not successful adapt or change

Encourage pupils to take responsibility for using strategies and newly learnt skills

Make/buy equipment & resources

(See pages 183–184 or order resources from the areas in Chapter 6)

↓

Introduce strategies and interventions to pupils and use them consistently

↑

Ensure that all staff are confident using strategies and interventions

←

Create a system for resource storage and accessibility

(See Language Area Stickers*)

←

* Stickers are available from www.languageforlearning.co.uk/shop

116

Attention and Listening Skills

Observed Behaviours:

A child may be observed:

- Finding it difficult to attend to the speaker
- Experiencing difficulty sitting still during whole-class teaching
- Not responding to instructions as part of a group or whole class
- Not asking questions, as used to not understanding, so does not question
- Being more able to engage when visual or kinaesthetic learning opportunities are presented
- Not always complying with instructions
- Relying on peers and copying their actions
- Being distracted by redundant information, i.e. extraneous noise
- Experiencing difficulty staying on task
- Requiring simplified instructions in order to understand

Positive Ways to Communicate

1   **Speak clearly** – give clear, short instructions and 'chunk' information. If you have an accent, be aware of regional terms you may use and how your phrasing may appear odd to your pupils. The larger the class, the slower you need to speak.

Be aware of how many key words are being used; e.g. 'Get your **number book** from your **drawer**; on a **clean page**, **write** the **date** and **draw a square**' contains at least nine key words, too many for most pupils with SLCN to understand.

2   **Secure the pupil's attention** before giving an instruction, for instance by calling his or her name.

3   **Avoid background noise** and be aware of distractions and try to eliminate or reduce them.

4 **Identify new vocabulary and explain it** – remember that pupils have had different levels of exposure to vocabulary. Terms not in everyday use need to be explained.

5 **Re-word key sentences** – complex sentences containing unfamiliar vocabulary may need to be re-worded.

6 **Explain idioms and non-literal language** as many pupils have difficulties understanding idioms such as, 'I'm tearing my hair out' or non-literal language such as 'I want you to work so hard there'll be steam coming off the paper.' It is, however, important to use this type of language as it is so much a part of our culture, but it must be explained.

7 **Ask pupils to repeat back what they have to do.** After giving the pupil an instruction, repeat the key words then ask the pupil to say these words back to you. When pupils have said words out loud they have more chance of remembering them.

8 **Position pupils so that eye contact can be maintained.** During discussion times arrange seating so that pupils can establish eye contact with each other as well as the adult. Encourage pupils to look at the speaker.

9 **Arrange seating so that concentration is maintained.** Position pupils who are easily distracted near you for class-level work and use screens to make a quieter area when working independently.

10 **Allow a variety of noise levels** in class – vary your acceptance of noise-level to meet the demands of different speaking and listening activities.

11 Use the **Ten-second Rule.** Give the pupil time to process what has been said by using the ten-second rule – once you have given an instruction allow the pupil 10 seconds to respond. During this time, consider the instruction: Were there too many words? Was the vocabulary too difficult to understand? If the pupil does not respond after 10 seconds, either rephrase the instruction or if the right level of language was used the first time, simply repeat the instruction again.

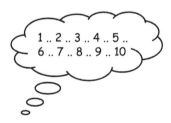

12 Use **positive statements** about what the pupil should do, e.g. say, 'Walk' rather than 'Don't run,' 'Look at me and think about what I'm saying' rather than 'Listen.'

13 **Praise good listening.** Say, 'Good looking at the speaker, Naseem' rather than focusing on the pupils who are distracted.

14 **Sequence instructions.** Give them in the same order as the action required, e.g. 'It's PE then break time', rather than 'Before break time it's PE.'

15 **Rehearse** – encourage pupils to 'rehearse' what they have heard by saying it over and over silently (this may have to be done out loud to begin with).

16 **Check understanding** by asking open-ended questions after information has been given, e.g. 'Which book do you have to use?' 'How are you going to start?'

17 **Name** – provide the words for familiar and unfamiliar actions, objects and concepts, 'We're **sketching**', 'Find England on the **globe**' or 'You are feeling **anxious.**'

18 Consider your **communication pace.** Speak slowly during conversations so that pupils have time to respond and take turns.

19 **Pause** frequently when talking and use an expectant expression so that pupils will be encouraged to actively participate and take turns in conversation.

20 **Confirm** – respond to pupils in a way that indicates that you have not only heard them but you have understood what they have said or what they intend.

21 **Comment** on what is happening as pupils are doing it, e.g. 'You are pouring the water into the container ready to do the floating and sinking activity.'

22 **Show a finished example** if you are asking pupils to make something they have not necessarily seen before. This will provide them with more understanding as they try to process what they have to do.

23 **Organise and label** equipment and storage areas to support organisational skills and understanding when pupils are asked to find/use unfamiliar equipment.

Universal Strategies and Approaches

24 Use **Visual cueing, gesture and/or signing** to accompany verbal instructions or information, e.g. have objects and pictures, illustrating topic work, to hand to illustrate new vocabulary or concepts. Be aware of visual recognition development – make sure that the visuals used are at the right level of development for your pupils.

25 **Active listening** – this approach breaks listening down into three skills – looking, sitting still and thinking (Johnson and Player 2009). This can be extended by showing pupils that in order to listen effectively they must look at the person who is talking, sit still, stay quiet so that everyone can listen and listen to all the words (Spooner and Woodcock 2010). Use picture cue cards to support pupils' understanding of each skill.

26 **Listener role play** – two adults demonstrate poor listening to the class encouraging pupils to call out, pantomime style, when they spot a poor listening behaviour such as not looking at the speaker, interrupting, fidgeting etc.

27 **Seeking clarification cue cards** help pupils to develop their ability to take responsibility for not understanding by creating a culture in the classroom that gives them the confidence to say if they, a) couldn't hear, b) didn't understand the words you used or c) had difficulty with the pace. Do this by specifically teaching them how to do it and praising them when they do.

28 **School routine cue cards** are illustrations representing simple routines or instructions used on a daily basis in school, e.g. General – yes, no, ok, wait, tidy up,

quiet, sit, share etc. Going to Assembly – line up, quiet, walk, sit etc. Getting Ready for PE – PE bag, shorts, top, trainers, tidy clothes, line up etc. Simply show the picture at the same time as giving the instruction.

29 **Visual timetables** help pupils understand what will be happening during the school day, to support the development of skills such as sequencing and recall and the understanding of specific time concepts, such as yesterday, last week, the day after tomorrow etc. They are also useful for reducing anxiety in pupils who need routine.

30 **Messenger** – give pupils a verbal message to give to another member of staff. The message should require an answer so that it is clear that it was delivered and/or relayed accurately. Giving pupils experience of being sent on errands to collect something from a cupboard or another room would also increase their ability to understand and remember instructions.

31 **Comic strips** – good for illustrating the main points of new information within a topic, support understanding and memory.

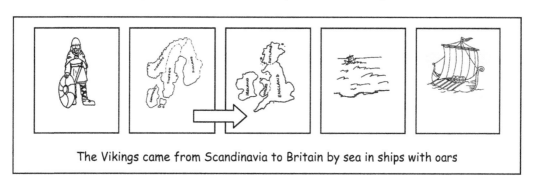

The Vikings came from Scandinavia to Britain by sea in ships with oars

32 **Task management boards** support pupils' ability to understand instructions and stay on task throughout an activity, whilst carrying the instructions by providing pictorial and or written support of the stages within a single activity.

For younger pupils:

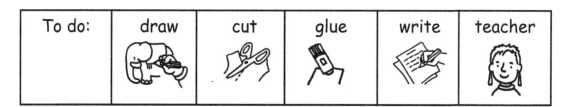

To do:	draw	cut	glue	write	teacher

For older pupils:

TASK MANAGEMENT BOARD	
Task: **Equipment:**	
1.	
2.	
3.	
4.	
5.	
I will be finished when:	**I can now:**

33 **Listen and clap** – read a passage, story or poem. Ask pupils to clap when they hear a specific word or sound, e.g. 'Roman' or 'sh'. Adapt to include specific information. For example, 'I want you to listen out for the types of food the Saxons eat and the games the children liked playing.' Different information could be listened for by different pupils, so varying the level of difficulty.

34 **Chinese whispers** work well whilst lining up for PE, playtime etc. Begin with very simple, short sentences using familiar vocabulary.

35 **Simon says** can be adapted as a cross curricular listening warm up with the level of difficulty increased as skills improve.

36 **Lesson warm up** – start the lesson with a short focusing activity, e.g. for maths count to 20 in 2s, for art and craft hold up items of equipment asking the class to mime the function, e.g. scissors – cutting action. This will help pupils to switch focus to a new topic and practise specific skills.

37 **Pair presenting** – use peer support through pair work. An able pupil presents a story or information to an audience whilst his or her partner (pupil with language difficulties) provides gesture or picture cue cards.

38 **Talk and question** – seat pupils so that they can all see each other. Ask each pupil in turn to tell the rest of the class something about themselves. When everyone has had a turn, ask questions like, 'What did Carl say?' or, 'Who went to Alton Towers?' Adapt this for news time. Direct each pupil to give one piece of news then ask the rest of the class to retell someone else's news, e.g. 'Gemma said she went to see her new baby in hospital'. Provide picture prompts for reluctant speakers.

Targeted Strategies and Approaches

39 **Speaker, listener, observer** – in groups of three the speaker tells the group about something, the listener re-tells the incident, then the observer comments on how much information the listener remembered. At first it is best if the speaker is an adult who keeps the narrative simple and within the pupils' experience. Later it is a useful group activity to reinforce information from current topic work.

40 **Picture prompting** – use photographs or symbols to develop the ability to process instructions. Select a group of pictures which belong together, e.g. children's clothes, then suggest an activity such as going to the beach for the day. Say to the pupils 'We are going to the beach for the day. It's hot so you will need to take your swimming things, a hat, an anorak and your flip-flops.' The pupils select these objects. Gradually increase the number of items you ask for and increase the level difficulty by including colour, shape and size. This strategy is easily adapted for use across the curriculum, e.g. 'Go to the sports hall and set out the following equipment, six hoops, six balls, six bean bags and six ropes.' Give the pupil(s) a photograph of how it should look, next time let them look at the photograph, but not take it with them and finally expect them to do it without a visual cue.

41 **Visualising** – ask pupils to imagine themselves doing what they have been asked to do, as they are being told. This could be supported by photographs or pictures. Start by asking for a simple description of something familiar, e.g. their front door, their favourite toy or a pet. Explain that they were imagining or visualising to be able to describe.

42 **Auditory discrimination ice-breakers** are activities that could be carried out at the start of group work. Consider the following suggestions:

1 Use commercial auditory discrimination resources

2 Record familiar sounds or well known voices from around the school and take photos for matching

3 Play 'Listen to the Silence' – sit very quietly whispering the names of the things that can be heard

4 Play an unfamiliar pop song, asking pupils what instruments they can hear or what lyrics they can remember

5 Play, 'Join in Clap' – one person claps a simple rhythm and each pupil joins in, in turn, until everyone is clapping the same rhythm.

6 Play, 'Copy Clap' – as above but each pupil claps in turn so that they practise remembering the rhythm.

43 **Recording devices** are useful for a) vital information so that pupils can listen repeatedly or for b) pupils to record their ideas so they will not be forgotten. Explore the following: Dragon software by Nuance; WriteOnline by Cricksoft; Communicate in Print by Widgit and Talking Tins by Taskmaster.

44 **Barrier games** are a brilliant way of getting pupils to practise communication skills. Put a screen between two pupils and introduce activities which require giving and receiving instructions. Use worksheets that contain pictures of current topic vocabulary – a diagram of a plant, the characters in a story or instruments in an orchestra for example. Each pupil has the same worksheet and an identical set of coloured pencils. The pupils takes it in turn to give an instruction such as, 'Colour the petal red' or 'Colour the violin blue' etc. Both pupils then carry out all of the instructions and the sheets are compared at the end. To start with it may be necessary to do this with an adult giving the instruction to a group of pupils.

45 **Home–school link books** support communication between pupils with SLCN and school staff. Missed opportunities for communication can arise because pupils may have difficulties remembering and sequencing information they want to relay or reporting on events that have happened at school or home. The link book is used to record information by both school staff and parents, such as, future events, current class topics and news. It can also be used to relay something that has happened to the child which was confusing, exciting, upsetting or a new experience. The pupil should see the book as a 'friend' so it is important that it is kept as neutral as possible and not used to report on the pupil's behaviour or academic performance in school.

Commercial Materials available from Language for Learning

- Listening cards, strips and flip books
- Seeking Clarification cards and flip books
- Going Home Task Management Board
- Investigating in Science flip book
- Instant Task Management Board
- Routine cards and flip books
- My Work board and cards
- Visual Timetable packs
- Tune Into series – Yellow Door
- Come Alive listening games and activity pack – Yellow Door
- Speaking and Listening Set – Yellow Door
- Early Listening Skills – Speechmark

Recommended Commercial Materials Available from Other Sources

Teaching Children to Listen – Featherstone Education

Listen Think and Do – LDA

Receptive Language Difficulties – LDA

WriteOnline – Cricksoft

Communicate in Print – Widgit Software

Listening Skills – LDA

Picture Sound Lotto – LDA

Good Listening Posters – Taskmaster

Look Hear! – LDA

The Language Gap – AMS Educational

Talking Tins – Taskmaster

Linguafun – Micas

Using Strategies at Home: Visual Timetable

STRATEGY	PARENTS	PUPIL	COMMENTS
			Make notes to improve/adapt the strategy – discuss with the SENCO or TA
Visual Timetable This will help to understand/develop: 1 What will happen next/during the day 2 What expectations there are 3 Abstract concepts related to time, e.g. first, second, third, last, next, today, tomorrow, yesterday, days of the week, date etc 4 General communication skills, i.e. attention skills, listening, commenting, questioning, discussing past and future events, recall and prediction 5 General organisational skills, i.e. top–bottom working and left–right working 6 Independent working	This timetable (with instructions) will be provided by school. Try to use it daily with your child. Provide similar timetables for activities/events at home, i.e. evening activities, school holidays etc.	Use your visual timetable so that you are ready for school. It will help you to have the right equipment for the right day, to ask questions about lessons and activities in advance so that you feel more confident to talk to your parents/friends about what has been interesting and what you like/don't like.	

Using Strategies at Home: Task Management Boards

STRATEGY	PARENTS	PUPIL	COMMENTS
Task Management Boards These work like a recipe, helping to complete tasks by listing equipment and the order in which to do things. They work because they: 1 Have less language to process 2 Reduce the load on memory 3 Develop organisational skills 4 Support independent working	An example will be given to you by school. Your child may bring a task management board home to help with getting ready for school. You can make them to help your child do things independently at home. Go through the strip to make sure that each step and the final result is understood. Help your child to move along from one stage to the next by referring to the strip. Move on to preparing the strip together, ask your child to guess what will be next on the strip. Once this has become familiar, encourage your child to use the strip independently.	Use task management boards so that your activities at home are easier to do. They will help you to find equipment, know exactly what you have to do and what to do first, second, third and so on.	Make notes to improve/adapt the strategy – discuss with the SENCO or TA

128

Using Strategies at Home: Home–school Link Book

STRATEGY	PARENTS	PUPIL	COMMENTS
Home–school Link Book This will help to: 1 Remember and sequence factual information 2 Report on events which have taken place 3 Interpret social situations 4 Make sense of new experiences and remember the 'how', 'what' and 'when' etc of homework	This will be provided by school. A teacher or TA will write about things to do with school and you can write about things to do with home so that it is easy to chat. The sort of things you will write about are: 1 Information about future events, topics and news, (e.g. we went to Alton Towers at the weekend and ….) 2 A quick summary of something that your child enjoyed/didn't enjoy 3 A social or behavioural situation that may have been confusing to him/her 4 A new experience that he/she had to deal with Your child should see this book as a 'friend' so it is important that it is kept as neutral as possible and not used as a way of reporting on their behaviour, their inability to cope or the problems you are having.	A home–school link book will make it easy for you to talk to your parents and teachers about things going on in your life. Your teachers and parents will not write anything that you do not want to talk about or you do not want everyone to know. Tell them what you would like to include and listen to their suggestions. You might like to attach things like brochures, tickets or photos.	Make notes to improve/adapt the strategy – discuss with the SENCO or TA

Understanding the Meaning of Words

Observed Behaviours:

A child may be observed:

- Having difficulty learning new vocabulary
- Experiencing difficulty understanding language – both at single word and sentence level
- Struggling to find the right word – hesitating, using a similar word, using gesture or mime to compensate or creating new words
- Confusing words belonging to the same semantic group, e.g. says 'yacht' for 'ship'; 'clock' for 'watch'
- Experiencing difficulties learning, retaining and then retrieving new vocabulary
- Learning a word in one situation but then experiencing difficulties applying it or generalising its use
- Experiencing difficulties defining words including identifying similarities or differences between word meanings
- Experiencing greater difficulty with more abstract concepts, i.e. time concepts – next week, last term, the day after tomorrow
- Being inflexible with language, e.g. becoming confused with words that have multiple meanings
- Having difficulty reading for meaning

Positive Communication

1   Think about the complexity of the vocabulary you are using – if it is new or difficult provide a **visual cue**.

2   **Label** – provide the words for familiar and unfamiliar actions, objects and concepts, 'We're **sketching**', 'Find England on the **globe**' or 'You are feeling **anxious**.'

3   **Reinforcement** – reinforce vocabulary by giving pupils experience of target words in as many different contexts and with as many different adults as possible. Link new vocabulary to concrete objects, use the words in role-play situations and illustrate with pictures or symbols.

4   Do not assume pupils understand **time concepts**. Keep conversation in the here and now, unless supported by visual information – see Visual Timetables in Attention and Listening p. 121.

5   **Generalise** – do not assume that pupils will generalise the use of vocabulary from one context to another – provide visual clues to help pupils to do this.

6   **Model** – reduce anxiety by not insisting on the correct word; be accepting of a description or a similar word, but use the correct word in your reply, e.g. 'It's got countries on it and its round.' 'Yes – it's the globe.'

7   **Cue in with sound** – some pupils may find it helpful if you cue them in first, with the initial sound, then the first syllable, then second syllable etc, e.g. 'an…angl…anglo…anglo sa…' etc. However, others may find this a distraction.

8   **Cue in with a phrase** made up of shorter words, e.g. 'It's water in a can – it's a …'(watering can). 'There's air round a plane – it's an …' (aeroplane). 'The book's in a case – it's a …' (bookcase). 'It's what you daub on the wall – it's …' (wattle and daub).

9   **Give pupils time** – during discussion times some pupils need time to recall the appropriate word – it may be helpful to move on to the next question with another pupil, asking the first pupil to let you know when he or she has remembered.

10   **Refer** – use the visual materials which support new vocabulary displayed on classroom walls by referring to them as you speak – pupils need reminding that they are there.

Universal Strategies and Approaches

11 **Be systematic** – adopt a systematic approach, e.g. 'Word Aware' (see Commercial Resources, p. 138) to teach new vocabulary. Choose both concrete and abstract concepts related to topic vocabulary and prioritise the vocabulary for pupils to understand or use.

Nouns	Functions	Categories	Attributes	Concepts
metal	touch	materials	hard	same
plastic	feel	natural	soft	different
wood	cut	man-made	rough	
paper	squeeze		smooth	
clay	bend			

12 Use a **What Is It? Board** designed to build word definition skills by asking questions related to the meaning of a word, for instance 'What do you do with it? Where do you find it? What sound does it begin with? How many syllables does it have? What does it rhyme with? What does it look/smell/taste like?' Make a board with a space for the target word (nouns work best) in the centre and the questions above placed around the sides. Make sure each question is colour- and picture-coded. Work round the board discussing the word in relation to the questions to help pupils gain a better understanding of what the word means.

Make **word definition cue cards** each with a different question from the What Is It? Board (symbol and colour coded) so that a range of activities can be introduced, e.g. in a small group give each pupil one of the cards. Place an object related to current topic work in the centre of the group and ask each pupil in turn to use the card to describe it.

13 Provide **picture and word boards** to support topic vocabulary for groups to refer to whilst listening to information containing new vocabulary, completing work in class or at home. Constantly refer to the board directing pupils to the appropriate picture as you speak. For more complex vocabulary provide visual or kinaesthetic boards exhibiting real materials, e.g. different textures.

14 **Abstract words** – using vocabulary from current topic work learn abstract words by linking them to known concrete words. For example, lay out large pictures representing, 'hospital', 'a nurse', 'an ambulance'. Place the words below onto cards and attach them to one or more of the pictures – solid, new, happy, tall, hungry, large, heavy, nervous, fast, loud.

15 Understanding and using words to do with concepts can be a struggle. These words are abstract, difficult to define and often change their meaning when used in different contexts, e.g. rough – rough road; feeling rough; rough and ready or left – left as a direction; left as a political movement or left as in forgotten. Consider making landscape-shaped **interactive concept posters** with a space for the concept word in the centre and four large frames (two on each side) to hold information about the word. Include the following headings: Experience – touch, taste, smell, feelings, event; Visualise – add pictures, photos, drawings, symbols; Explain – talk about the concept; Define – look the word up in a visual dictionary and record definition. For more ideas look in the 'Speech, Language and Communication Pocketbook' Mason and Milne (2014).

16 **Reinforce the meaning** of the word not just the label or name, for example, 'It's a **plant**, you find it in the **garden** and it **grows**.'

17 **Check understanding** by asking open-ended questions after information has been given, e.g. 'Which book do you have to use?'

18 **Identify differences** – develop an awareness of 'same' and 'different' to support an understanding of new vocabulary, e.g. the attributes that make a cat a cat and not a dog.

19 **Circumlocute** – encourage pupils to use circumlocution, i.e. to tell you all about the word, e.g. child: 'It's the thing in the PE shed with orange netting and posts and …' adult: 'Oh yes, the goalposts.' This strategy helps facilitate word retrieval.

20 **Identify word associations** when introducing vocabulary by using the word in a sentence or with another word that it is closely associated to, e.g. 'A bungalow is a house with no stairs, your Grandma's house is a bungalow.'

21 **Be meaningful** – teach new vocabulary in meaningful learning situations, using real objects and tapping into visual, auditory and kinaesthetic learning styles.

22 **Sentence clues** – teach words in sentences rather than in isolation, e.g. "We heat the room with a ...' (radiator). 'We go out to play when we hear the ...' (bell). "Egyptians live on the ..." (Nile). Where possible cue in with a picture.

23 **Pre-teach** – provide pre-teaching opportunities. Use topic books or revision guides from a lower key stage so that information can be 'scaffolded' from simple to more difficult.

24 **Word webs** are useful to demonstrate how words are linked.

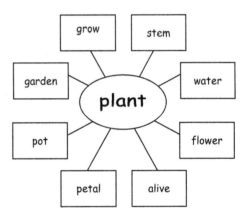

25 **Mind maps** provide visual semantic links between words. Arrange topic displays as a mind map on classroom walls. Provide simple mind maps of each curriculum topic and teach students to record their own work in mind map form. Use mind mapping to gather information about what students know before introducing a new topic. Mind map again once the topic is completed and compare the difference with pupils to illustrate how much they have learned.

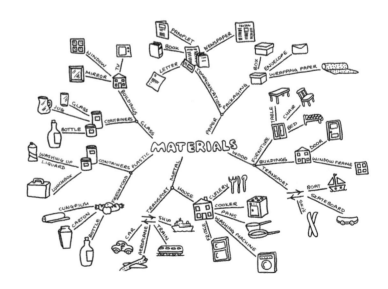

26 **Talking glossaries** – use tablets to download pictures, text and the spoken word to create talking glossaries of cross curricular vocabulary.

27 **Personal word books**, organised by category, help pupils to see how words are linked and therefore stored and retrieved more effectively. When pupils request a spelling, rather than asking for the initial sound, ask them to find the category that the word belongs to. The word is then recorded with related words which helps pupils to both understand the meaning of the word and also store it more effectively in his or her long-term memory. Choose about 15 categories to begin with and provide both the picture and the word. Stick these throughout the word book to create sections. An index can be created on the inside front cover and first page with an identical set of pictures to those pasted in the book.

28 **Commercial visual dictionaries** are easier than traditional dictionaries (arranged alphabetically) for pupils with SLCN to use. This is because they support understanding through pictures and categorisation rather than using language to define language.

29 **Colour coding** is useful in grouping related words to develop concept knowledge. For example, in science all things to do with heat could be red, everything to do with growth green. In maths colour all words to do with addition red, subtraction yellow, multiplication blue etc.

30 **Visual timelines** can be placed around the classroom with the important events in the school year clearly marked. Include holidays, special activities, children's birthdays and social events. Attach a moveable arrow pinpointing the current day. Refer to it regularly, reinforcing time concept vocabulary.

Targeted Strategies and Approaches

31 **Be relevant** – do not give SLCN pupils more words to learn than the rest of the class. This can happen if they are involved in a language group. Always work on vocabulary that is currently being used in the classroom or words that are related to their home, family, school or local community.

32 **Involve parents and carers** by providing lists of forthcoming topic vocabulary, with some ideas on how to reinforce the meaning of the words across different contexts at home. Plan well in advance of the topic being introduced in school.

33 **Which one?** – place a collection of objects, pictures or words from current topic work in front of a small group of pupils. Describe one of the objects, asking pupils to guess what it is. Gradually involve pupils as the describers.

34 Play versions of **'I went to market and I bought …'** depending on the topic vocabulary you want to teach. For example, first pupil: 'I'm going to paint a picture so I will need an apron.' Second pupil, 'I'm going to paint a picture so I will need an apron and some water.' This can be extended to add a reason why each thing introduced is needed.

35 Play **Snap** and **Pelmanism**, matching words and word definitions with pictures.

36 Play **I spy** targeting topic vocabulary and using a description rather than a letter name, e.g. 'I spy with my little eye something that is brown, square, has a shoulder strap and contains something to help me breathe during an air raid.'

37 Play an adapted version of **Pass the parcel** – put objects or pictures representing the vocabulary you are teaching between the layers of paper in your parcel. When the music stops the player holding the parcel unwraps a layer, names the picture or the object and says one thing about it. If the information is accurate he or she keeps the picture/object. The winner has the most pictures/objects at the end of the game.

38 Explore **matching** by cutting pictures of current topic vocabulary in half then arranging them randomly on a table so that pupils can find and match the two halves naming each picture as they match. Start with objects that are dissimilar then gradually introduce ones that are more difficult to sort from each other.

39 **Sorting and classifying**, often neglected as children leave reception but a very useful strategy to support pupils' understanding and memory of new vocabulary. Use as many objects, pictures and ways of sorting as possible.

Start with just two classifications, i.e. 'gas and not gas', 'liquid and not liquid' or 'solids and not solids', increase to 'gas and liquid', then to 'gas, liquid and solids'.

40 **Describing 1** – once pupils understand the function and location of objects, teach them how to describe. To begin with, practise using two elements only – size and colour, e.g. 'It's big and blue.' Gradually add words linked to the senses – 'What does it look like?', 'What does it feel like?', 'What does it sound like?', 'Does it have a taste?', 'Does it have a smell?' The 'Word Association Cards' (see Commercial Resources, p. 138) are useful for this.

41 **Describing 2** – using cue cards as described above give one to each pupil then pass an object round. As each pupil receives the object he or she thinks of a word to describe it from the cue card they have, e.g. object – a magnet, first pupil has the colour cue card and her response is, 'Silvery grey with red tips' the next student has the 'size' card and says, 'Small and chunky.' Gradually increase expectation so that the cue card word and the description are included and the pupil is repeating what has been said before, for example, 'The magnet is silvery grey with red tips and is small and chunky.'

42 **Describing 3** – pass a picture or object related to current topic work around the group. As each pupil receives it they a) add a word to describe it, b) explain what it could be used for and c) offer something that it is associated with.

43 **Describing 4** – pupils take it in turns to describe a person, object or place from their current topic for the rest of the group to guess. The 'describer' is given a picture of the person/object/place and a cue card listing a range of associations to help with the description (function, location, parts, category, starts with, rhymes with, has ... syllables, sounds like, smells like, shape, colour, size etc).

44 **Describing 5** – select pupils for different activities by description, e.g. 'If you have sisters go to the printing table' or 'All pupils with blonde hair go to the model-making table unless you have brown eyes.' The level of difficulty will depend on the pupils you are targeting.

45 Provide **Flow diagrams** to support sequencing skills, e.g. a seed growing into a plant, the construction of an Anderson Shelter, etc.

46 Match selling **slogans** to different types of shops or products, e.g. fresh fish, juicy fruits, mouth-watering melons, crunchy crisps, shiny shoes etc.

Recommended Commercial Resources from Language for Learning

- Word Association cards – Language for Learning
- 'What Is It?' boards and posters – Language for Learning
- 'What Is It?' category and attribute spinners – Language for Learning
- Maths Concept Wheel – Language for Learning
- Transport: Where do I go? – Language for Learning
- Animals: Where do I live? – Language for Learning
- Developing Language Concepts – Speechmark
- Word Aware – Speechmark
- Same/Different flip book – Smartkids
- Antonyms/Homonyms/Synonyms – Smartkids
- Smartchute and cards (opposites, things that go together, the house, collective nouns, following instructions, idioms, omonyms) – Smartkids
- 'What Would You Take?' flip book – Smartkids
- Cryptic Compounds – Smartkids
- Talk About series (Things we do, Things at home, How we feel, Things outside) – Yellow Door

---

Recommended Commercial Materials Available from Other Sources

- The Visual Dictionary – Dorling Kindersley
- Oxford Junior Illustrated Dictionary – Oxford University Press
- Oxford Junior Illustrated Thesaurus – Oxford University Press
- Kidspiration – SEMERC
- Google Earth
- Basic Verbs Colour Cards – Speechmark
- Nouns – LDA
- Conceptual Language Chatterbox – LDA
- Fun Decks – Taskmaster
- Triple Talk Vocabulary Cards – Taskmaster
- Talking Tins – LDA

Using Strategies at Home: What Is It? Board

STRATEGY	PARENTS	PUPIL	COMMENTS Make notes to improve/adapt the strategy – discuss with the SENCO or TA
What Is It? Board The What Is It? Board is a way of teaching your child new words. Words are best taught in a systematic way and revised frequently. This board helps to do this by linking the word to its associations.	Your school will provide you with a board, the words your child is learning at the moment, a picture to represent each word and a sentence or two to say what it means. This is what you do: 1 Say the word. 2 Look at the picture of the word and place it in the centre of the What is it? Board. 3 Now work round the board discussing each section. Function – what does it do, what is it used for? Location – where do we find it? Where does it live? What parts does it have? and What category does it belong to? Ask your child to clap out the syllables of the word, to think of some rhyming words (these can be real or nonsense words) followed by the sound the word starts with. Continue by thinking about its attributes – smell, taste, colour, shape etc and finally what feelings you have about it. 4 Now think about the meaning of the word and help your child to say what the word means, talk about different situations the word is used in and then put the word into a sentence. 5 Put the picture and word up in your child's bedroom or on the fridge and revise it regularly.	This is a fun way to learn new words – it will help your parents too because they will not know all of them. There may be words you hear to do with out of school activities – get an adult to write them down and practise learning them this way too.	

Using Strategies at Home: Mind Mapping

STRATEGY	PARENTS	PUPIL	COMMENTS
Mind Mapping Mind mapping is useful as it reduces language load to single key words, each representing an element of the concept being learnt. A mind map is an efficient memory jogger; the key words are readily expanded into sentences and the sentences into paragraphs. So, in summary, mind mapping supports our language skills in a number of ways by: 1 Recording information logically and linking it to what is already known. 2 Grouping vocabulary in a way that helps to understand it, store it in our long term memory and remember it when we need it. 3 Helping to think of sentences and a plot when using it for story writing.	Your school will provide you with some examples. 1 Use coloured pencils or felts. 2 Choose a picture/word to go in the centre (the category name or topic title, e.g. rivers). 3 Draw four or five 'main roads' away from this central picture/word each in a different colour. 4 Label these roads with the names and pictures of the main categories of the topic, (e.g. weather system – evaporation, condensation, precipitation). 5 From each of these draw 'minor roads' again labelled with pictures/words to do with these sub categories, (e.g. sun, heat, clouds, rain). A mind map can be completed in one go or built up over a period of time. Encourage your child to draw the images, use colour and print the words. There are computer programmes available to construct mind maps – search 'Tony Buzan'.	Mind maps are a great way to get lots of information down on paper quickly and in a fun way. They also help you to understand what you have written down and give you a useful way of revising for exams. Practise by making mind maps of your family tree, the different parts of your life, your favourite things on TV etc.	

141

Using Strategies at Home: Word Books

STRATEGY	PARENTS	PUPIL	COMMENTS Make notes to improve/adapt the strategy – discuss with the SENCO or TA
Word Books These are personal banks of words arranged in categories (i.e. people, places, actions, feelings etc) rather than alphabetically. The category names and the number of categories used are flexible and depend on age and ability. This type of word book/dictionary helps pupils see how words are linked together by association. Each time it is used the pupil considers what the word means and is reminded of other words, which are of course recorded in the same section, that are related to it. This strategy helps pupils to store words and remember them when they are needed.	Your child may bring a word book/file from school. If not get him/her a small note book file (A5 portrait is good). Ask school for copies of category pictures. Choose about 15 categories depending on your child's ability. You will need two sets. Discuss what each of the pictures represents. Stick one set on the inside cover and first page to form an index. The other set is divided throughout the book and placed one on the top right hand corner of each category section. As your child asks for the spelling of the word, say 'What is it?'/ 'Where does it belong?' and help him/her select the category from the index. The word is written on the page – adding a drawing can help with understanding and finding the word at another time. Arrange the words in alphabetical order on the category page if you wish.	Your own 'Word Book' helps you with understanding the meaning of words and with spelling. It is also useful if you can't think of the right word to use. Always have it with you and don't be afraid to ask adults to write words for you.	

Structure and Rules: Syntax

Observed Behaviours:

A child may be observed:

- Using immature expressive language – missing words from sentences, confusing the word order or using the wrong word endings
- Misunderstanding instructions or questions that contain negatives, pronouns, plurals and tenses
- Speaking telegrammatically, i.e. using only the key words needed to convey a message
- Struggling to understand complex grammatical structures, such as connectives – and, so, but, to
- Making grammatical errors in written work
- Struggling to sequence ideas and thoughts so has difficulty recalling events in the correct sequence or telling a story in the correct sequence

Positive Communication

1 **Speak clearly** – if you have a different regional accent, be aware of unfamiliar terms you may use and how your phrasing may appear odd to your pupils. The larger the class, the slower you need to speak.

2 **Keep sentences short and 'chunk' information.** Reduce the number of clauses and keep in the correct sequence, e.g. 'The Vikings had 16 letters in their alphabet. These letters were called runes. There were not enough runes for every sound in the Viking language. This made spelling very difficult.' Rather than, 'The 16 runes, the letters in the Viking alphabet, made spelling difficult because there weren't enough for every sound in their language.'

3 **Simplify words and sentences** or repeat using a more simplified version, e.g. 'Specific foods are good for growth, others for energy – some foods are good for helping you to grow others for helping you to run and play sports.'

4   **Avoid correcting pupils' poor grammar**; rather emphasise the correct form when replying, e.g. 'Her give me the wrong book Miss,' 'Oh **she gave** you the wrong book did she?' When working on increasing the level of grammatical difficulty with the pupil, stress the key words but retain normal speech intonation.

5   **Extending** – encourage pupils to **extend** their sentences by repeating what the child said and adding extra syntactic or semantic information, e.g. child says 'it's big and round', adult responds, 'yes it's a big, round shiny ball'.

6   Introduce **visual support** to help pupils understand which elements are needed within a sentence.

7   **Memory** – be aware that the understanding of grammatical expression is closely linked to the ability to remember what has been said. Work on increasing pupils' ability to understand by using concrete objects. Make sure that they have a chance to familiarise themselves with the objects being used so that an immediate link is made with the object and the instruction.

Universal Strategies and Approaches

8   **Tense 1** – work on tense in relation to time using hand gestures. Place your left hand in front of you to indicate now/present, move it to your left hand side to indicate before/past, and move it to the right to indicate after/future, etc. Don't forget to reverse this if you are facing pupils.

9 **Tense 2** – work on tense by adapting stories or poems with repetitive dialogue for class choral speaking, e.g. 'The Gingerbread Man' – change 'Run, run as fast as you can, you can't catch me I'm the Gingerbread Man' to 'He ran and ran as fast as a van but he couldn't catch me I'm the Gingerbread Man'.

10 **Puppets** are useful to encourage shy pupils to talk. Start off with a simple dialogue between the adult and the puppet, gradually extending this to a dialogue between the adult's puppet and the child's puppet and eventually to a group of pupils with puppets.

11 Use **scripting** – a strategy that provides a sequence for the pupil to talk about an activity or routine that is familiar to them, e.g. 'Tell me about swimming – start in school – what happens first? How do you get there? What do you do before you go in the water?' etc.

12 Consider introducing **group speaking or chanting** to a range of topics. Group speaking gives pupils the opportunity to practise the use of complex grammar and chanting mnemonics, dates linked to facts, information from science has the added benefit of supporting long-term memory.

13 **Sentence work** – have a set of boxes available in the classroom labelled with basic elements of a sentence, for instance people, actions, objects, places, adjectives. Collect pictures linked to topic work to go in each box. The pupil selects a picture from a selection of the boxes, e.g. a person, an action and an object then organises these pictures in sequence to make a sentence – 'The woman is putting grey paint around her eyes.' Through questioning this can then be expanded to – 'The Egyptian woman is outlining her eyes with grey paint called kohl which looks pretty and also keeps flies away.'

Start early sentence construction using the following as a guideline:

Subject + verb/object	e.g. Dan walks or Dan has a bike
Question + object/verb	e.g. Who has a book? or Who is running?
Subject + verb + object	e.g. Maisie is catching the ball
Question + verb + object	e.g. Who is waving a flag?
Question + verb + place	e.g. Who is walking to school?

14 Improve **narrative skills** by working on shared stories or reports in small groups. The adult starts a familiar story or a report about a recent visit or visitor finishing in mid-sentence, each pupil, in turn, continues the story or report stopping when the adult raises his or her hand, until it is finished. As pupils become more confident the activity could be recorded to support written work.

Targeted Strategies and Approaches

15 **Technology** – take advantage of recording devices so that pupils can record story ideas before constructing sentences. This often works well with mind mapping.

16 Use **writing planners or frames** across the curriculum – these are reminder cue cards/sheets that range from very simple to fairly complex. A simple version may include key question words, i.e. **What? Where? Who?** together with a sequential set of questions linked to either a practical task, e.g. recording an activity, writing up an out of school trip, or a piece of writing.

17 **Acting out stories** – use small world play figures to act out simple stories, rather like children do when play acting with dolls. As each 'person' in the story talks or does something, move the appropriate piece.

18 **Story planners** – these are planning sheets that include a box to record what the story is about; they have beginning, middle and end areas containing questions such as 'When?' 'Who?' 'Where?' 'What happened?' 'How did they feel?' etc.

19 **Talking frames** support pupils when they are addressing the class. Pictures provide prompts for content and symbols for delivery, e.g. slow, loud etc. Include a beginning, middle and end.

20 **Questions** – develop your questioning skills so that you encourage thinking. Grade your use of question words from easy to hard – 'Who' 'What' 'When' 'Where' before 'How' and 'Why'. Use symbol cue cards representing each one for pupils who find them confusing.

21 **Open Questioning** – ask open questions, e.g. rather than asking 'did you go to the park?' ask the child to tell you about the park, what they did and what they saw.

22 Play Snap or Pelmanism matching **formal or informal sentences**, e.g. 'Hello Sally' with 'Hi Sal'.

23 Play Snap or Pelmanism to encourage the use of **plurals**. Make a set of matching pairs of cards; spread them face down on the table; in turn, two cards are turned over if a matching pair is turned over the player says, 'There are two …', if not the player says, 'There is one cat and one dog.' Again introduce pictures to do with current topic work.

24 **Emphasise** – practise simple sentences with different voices and emphasis, e.g. **I** like strawberries and cream.

> I **like** strawberries and cream.
> I like **strawberries** and cream.
> I like strawberries **and cream**.

25 **Pronouns 1** – work on pronouns by making two circles of card, one with a picture of a boy and one with a girl. Create a selection of cards each with a picture of either a boy or a girl performing an action. Encourage pupils to put the cards into the correct circle, saying, 'She's sleeping' or 'He's swimming' etc.

26 **Pronouns 2** – in a small group ask each pupil to say something about him or herself in turn. The pupil to the left repeats what has been said using the correct pronoun, e.g. 'My hair is black,' next pupil 'Her hair is black.' This pupil then continues.

27 **Grammar 1** – play 'Leave the person standing': ask the class to stand up, describe a member of the class, after each sentence the children who do not fit the description sit down, e.g. 'This person has blue eyes' all children with brown or green eyes sit down. As the class gets used to the game introduce more complex grammar, e.g. 'This person is sitting near the cupboard and in between two people with brown hair' etc.

28 **Grammar 2** – play 'Simon Says' using fairly complicated grammar, e.g. 'Before you touch your head cough,' 'If there's a girl in this class called Anne jump.'

29 Play **'Reporters'** – sit pupils in a circle; the first pupil whispers something he or she has done that day to the pupil on the left; that pupil then reports what has been said to the rest of the class, using the past tense. Model the reply, e.g. 'Matt said that he had ....'

Commercial Resources from Language for Learning

- Story Writing Cards – Language for Learning
- Early Story Writing – Language for Learning
- Crazy Fables – Smartkids
- Story Starter Cards - Smartkids
- Story Spinners – Smartkids
- Sentence Spinners – Smartkids
- Writer's Directory – Smartkids

Recommended Commercial Materials Available from Other Sources

- Range of Narrative resources for Key Stage 1–Key Stage 2 – Black Sheep Press
- Auditory Processing of WH Words – Taskmaster
- BROGY Sentence Builder – Taskmaster
- Preposition Overlays – Taskmaster
- Talking in Sentences – Taskmaster
- Grammar Game Boards – Taskmaster
- Teaching Grammar, Punctuation and Spelling through Drama (KS 2) – Brilliant Publications
- How to Dazzle at Grammar – Brilliant Publications
- How to Sparkle at Grammar and Punctuation – Brilliant Publications
- Ask and Answer Game Boards – Taskmaster

Structure and Rules: Phonology

Observed Behaviours:

A child may be observed:

- Struggling to make themselves understood, with unintelligible speech
- Experiencing difficulty blending sounds
- Substituting or missing sounds from words
- To have poor phonological awareness, i.e. sound knowledge of a word
- Experiencing difficulties learning new words, i.e. storing the sounds for a new word incorrectly, resulting in inaccurate use

Positive Communication

30 **Be honest** – do not pretend to understand a pupil if he or she is unintelligible. They usually know that you have not understood and it makes them feel that what they have to say is not important. Rather, ask for a repetition, using different words; the pupil will then know that he or she is worth communicating with.

31 **Repeating sounds** – try not to ask pupils to repeat sounds back to you correctly. This will have little long-term effect. For instance, whilst speaking to a Scottish person you were asked to repeat the word 'loch' with a Scottish accent, you would have little difficulty; however if you were then expected to pronounce the 'ck' sound in that way whenever it cropped up in a word you would find it very difficult.

32 **Modelling 1** – encourage children to listen to you modelling and emphasising target sounds, e.g. pupil says, 'Look it a nake', you respond "Yes it'**sssss** a **sssss**nake.'

33 **Modelling 2** – it is important to pronounce the individual sounds of speech in their pure form. It is a common mistake to add a vowel sound, e.g. 'feh' for 'f'. Ask pupils to look at your mouth so they can see how you are forming the sound.

34 When playing phonological games avoid using words with clusters, such as st/sk/sl/sm/sn/tr/fl/cl/gr/pr, instead **use consonant–vowel–consonant** words, e.g. hat, van, mop, pig etc.

Universal Strategies and Approaches

35 **Rhythm** – spend as much time as possible developing a sense of rhythm. Start with single beats, using clapping, tapping, shakers etc to accompany simple tunes, extend to more complex tunes and words – one beat per syllable.

36 **Rhyming** is a phonological skill that plays an important part in developing word knowledge. Always consider the rhyming element when teaching new words, for example, petal – metal, kettle etc. Nonsense words are fine to use if it is difficult to link with real words, e.g. scarab (as in Egyptian beetle) could be rhymed with plarab, barab, harab etc.

37 **Initial sounds** are obviously important – continue discussions about what words begin with beyond Reception and Key Stage 1 as often pupils with phonological awareness difficulties fail to hear the beginning and endings of words.

38 Play **'Initial sound rhythm'**. Start pupils off by saying something in rhythm like, 'Click, clack, clock.' The children join in, in turn, by using the same rhythm but changing the initial sound, e.g. 'Sick, sack, sock." To make this easier at first, give each child a card featuring an initial sound or blend. Some pupils may need to be partnered with a more able pupil.

39 **Phonology and understanding** – always link 'phonological awareness' and 'sound knowledge' to pupils' understanding of the meaning of words. This is best done when teaching new vocabulary, e.g. 'What does the word rhyme with?' 'How many syllables does it have?' 'What sound does it start with?' (see the What Is It? Board – strategy 12 in the Understanding the Meaning of Words section p. 132)

40 Work on segmentation by clapping out the **syllables** in words, highlighting them in different colours or providing pupils with word puzzles where each syllable is written on a different card and has to be joined to make the word.

41 Help pupils to **discriminate** between the sounds in words by discussing what is the same and what is different, e.g. target word – 'vapour'. 'Does it start with the same sound as voice?' 'Does it have the same number of sounds as paper?' etc.

42 Encourage pupils to **blend** sounds together to form words, e.g. bar + k = bark, sk + ip = skip etc.

Targeted Strategies and Approaches

43 **Combine auditory and visual stimuli** – use toys and equipment e.g. a music box, wind chimes, toy animals, cars and trains etc. Imitate the sound made by the toy and pupils may well join in. Encourage them to associate the object with its sound. For example, 'Fetch the one that goes oink, oink.'

44 **Discuss sounds** – cue pupils into events that are always associated with sound. For example, the sound of cutlery rattling, water being poured into a cup, keys jangling to open a door. Talk about what is happening when that sound is being made.

45 Play **'Where is that noise?'** – blindfold a pupil and make a sound from different parts of the room. The pupil has to point in the direction the sound is coming from. Vary the types of sounds being made.

46 **Sound lotto** – Use commercial auditory discrimination games such as 'Picture Sound Lotto' (see Commercial Resources at the end of this section) or record the voices of children in the group and play them back so that the rest of the group can point to the child whose voice they can hear. Familiar sounds around the school can also be recorded and linked to pictures cut from catalogues or taken with a digital camera.

47 **Barrier activity 1** – use a screen to play guessing games: the teacher or a pupil stands behind the screen, which hides a set of percussion instruments from the class. These are played and the rest of the class responds by describing what they hear, e.g. high, low, loud, scratchy, soft etc.

48 **Barrier activity 2** – again using a barrier and a collection of everyday objects ask the pupil to guess which one the sound is coming from.

49 Barrier activity 3 – help pupils to match sounds by providing two identical sets of shakers made up of five different sounds, e.g. use ten plastic water bottles and half-fill two with rice, two with sand, two with dried peas, two with beads and two with small pebbles. Then place one set of shakers behind a barrier and the other set in front of the targeted pupil. An adult or pupil behind the screen shakes one of the shakers and the target pupil has to find the shaker that makes the same sound. This can be simplified by starting with only two or three different sounds. It's also a good idea to colour code the shakers so that the 'match' can be checked easily.

50 Play **clapping activities**. In a small group one person starts a simple clapping rhythm then each pupil joins in, in turn, until each everyone is clapping the same rhythm. Extend to clapping out sounds in words, syllables in words, words in sentences.

51 **Listen to the silence** is a good activity for auditory discrimination. In a quiet classroom pupils listen for any sounds they can hear, whispering the name of the sounds when they hear them. Pupils could also listen out for their name whispered by the teacher. All pupils have to be quiet and still. When they hear it they can move to another part of the classroom.

52 Spot the difference 1 – develop pupils' ability to discriminate between similar sounds by using a set of large pictures that illustrate single syllable words with voiced and unvoiced initial blends, e.g. a key and a bee. In pantomime style, hold up the picture of the key and say, 'Is this some tea?' to which the class replies 'No it's a key.' Extend this to include word endings, e.g. 'Is this some soup?' 'No it's a suit.'

53 Spot the difference 2 – encourage pupils to distinguish between similar sounds by providing a picture board and asking pupils to point to the picture that begins with, for example the 'm' sound. Make sure there are also pictures of things beginning with the similar 'n' sound etc.

54 Morphology – pupils with phonological difficulties find it difficult to discriminate between word endings and as these indicate possession, plurals, the verb form or a change in tense the meaning can become obscured. Try to include word variations in word books and on displays, e.g. a **plant**, two **plants**, Imran is **planting** a tree and the tree has been **planted**.

Commercial Resources from Language for Learning

- Sounds Into Words – Language for Learning
- Tune Into Series – Yellow Door
- Cryptic Compounds – Smartkids

Recommended Commercial Resources from Other Sources

- Phonemic Awareness Key Stage 1 – Black Sheep Press
- How to Sparkle at Phonics – Brilliant Publications
- Soundtracks – Living and Learning
- Picture Sound Lotto – LDA
- Look Hear! – LDA
- Find the Rhyme – LDA
- Rhyme Lotto – TES Connect
- I Hear With My Little Ear – LDA
- Alphabet Soundtracks – Living and Learning
- Ladybug, Ladybug – LDA
- Slug in a Jug – Orchard Toys
- The I-Spy Game – Galt Toys
- Silly Bulls – Winslow Press

Social Communication Skills

Observed Behaviours:

A child may be observed:

- Lacking flexibility in use of language for a range of social functions, e.g. to share information, to comment, to express feelings, to make a suggestion
- Experiencing difficulties with conversational skills, including:
  - Waiting for and taking a turn in a conversation
  - Initiating and then maintaining a topic of conversation appropriately. A child may have a tendency to talk about a favourite topic
  - Repairing a breakdown when there is a misunderstanding
  - Awareness of the listener's knowledge, providing either too much or too little information for the listener to understand
- Finding it difficult to understand and use non-verbal communication skills, including eye contact, facial expressions, posture and proximity. A child may stand too close to others without realising the implications of this
- Speaking too loudly for the situation or using an inappropriate volume, intonation or unusual voice
- Taking the adult's role
- Talking at people rather than to them
- Not understanding hidden meaning or intent, i.e. making a literal interpretation of what has been said. A lack of use of intent or implied meaning results in a child appearing overly honest or 'blunt'. They may find it difficult to understand jokes or sarcasm
- Struggling to adapt and use language in a flexible way across different social situations

Positive Communication

1   Do not assume anything. Constantly **check understanding** especially in social situations.

2 **Be a good role-model** – the way you interact with colleagues, pupils and parents may be copied by your pupils with social communication needs because they do not understand that rules for children are not always observed by adults. E.g. talking in a loud voice to a colleague during quiet time.

3 **Make rules explicit** using peers as role models. Consistently identify what the pupil should **do** rather than should not do and record rules visually. Pupils with severe social communication difficulties respond more readily if adults say, 'The rule is ...' rather than 'I want you to ...' or 'You must ...'

4 Give pupils **genuine reasons to communicate** as language develops from the need to interact with others. Provide opportunities for that need, e.g. pupil struggling to put his coat on – do not rescue immediately, wait for him to indicate to you that he needs help. Model the correct way to ask from the simple to the more complex, e.g. 'Help,' 'Help me,' 'Help me with my coat,' 'Help me to put my coat on please.'

5 **Signal changes in topic**, e.g. 'We are now talking about the Romans.'

6 During discussion time **do not follow tangential replies** – re-direct the pupil back to the current topic of conversation, e.g. 'We're not talking about trains now we're talking about how our stomach works.'

7 **Check ambiguity** – before questioning the child's behaviour, check that the instruction given was not ambiguous and that the child's response was not simply a reaction to a literal interpretation or an inability to understand implied meaning, e.g. the child is told to put the writing underneath the picture – meaning 'below'. The child lifts up his stuck down picture, writes underneath then re-sticks the picture on top – very frustrating but the child was doing exactly what he or she had been told to do.

8 **Praise appropriate behaviour** rather than draw attention to inappropriate behaviour.

9 **Simplify language**, particularly within cause and effect situations, e.g. 'You hurt Robert so he feels angry and upset.'

10 **Responsive listening** – useful when pupils are emotionally distressed this strategy is a way of responding so that frustration is lowered rather than heightened. We all have difficulty expressing ourselves when emotions are running high, but for a pupil with SLCN this is a particularly difficult time. This is done by calmly 'echoing', in a neutral voice, what the distressed child's emotion appears to be rather than asking questions, giving advice or offering a solution. E.g. 'You're very angry/upset.' rather than 'Stop that, it isn't going to get you anywhere.'

11 **Jokes and sarcasm** – be careful when joking or using sarcasm, you may be taken literally. Make sure to explain what you mean when using ambiguous language. Use resources that interpret non-literal language such as 'What Did You Say? What Do You Mean?' – see Commercial Resources, p. 162.

12 **Confirm** that you have heard what he or she has said positively; 'Mm' or a nod may not be understood.

13 **Comment** – work or play alongside pupils making comments rather than asking questions. Pupils with social communication needs find this less threatening and will be encouraged to start making comments of their own.

14 **Ask open ended questions**, e.g. 'Tell me about your picture,' rather than 'Have you drawn a castle?' This will help to produce a dialogue rather than just 'yes/no' answers.

15 **Praise and criticism** – pupils with social communication needs often find it difficult to receive praise or criticism. Make comments specific and honest by selecting the positive, e.g. 'That's good – you've illustrated your work well and used some very good words' rather than 'Well done, Anna' or 'That's lifelike because the shading is making the figure look nice and round. You can work on the face detail next time' rather than, 'Great Alex – now try to get the face right.'

Pupils with social communication skills also find it difficult to give praise or criticism as they tend to be bluntly honest. Include opportunities in social communication skills groups to work on a simple formula such as, say something good first then suggest an improvement etc. Provide helpful phrases and discuss when they might apply. Revise regularly.

Universal Strategies and Approaches

16 **Taking responsibility for not understanding** – create a culture in the classroom that gives pupils the confidence to say if they, a) couldn't hear, b) didn't understand the words you used or c) had difficulty with the pace. Do this by specifically teaching them how to do it and praising them when they do. 'Seeking Clarification Cue Cards', strategy 27 in Attention and Listening, are useful for this.

17 Use **volume control** symbol cards to support pupils who find it difficult to speak at an appropriate volume. E.g. each card has a photograph or picture of a situation or location with a highlighted volume control bar at the bottom. They can be used as a reminder in real situations or for group role play or discussion activities. Snap or Pelmanism cards could also be created so that an activity could be devised matching the volume indicator to the situation or location. Large versions of the cards could also be placed around the school.

18 Work on **understanding the rules of sports and games**. Ensure that pupils with poor memory and sequencing skills have the opportunity to learn rules thoroughly even if this has to be done one-to-one or in a small group.

19 **Jokes** – pupils with SLCN often struggle to tell and understand jokes. Provide opportunities for them to practise telling and or discussing jokes, e.g. Make a cardboard TV screen: pupils take it in turns to tell jokes from the screen at the end of each day.

20 **Why do people not always tell the truth** – spend time discussing the types of situations when it is probably not a good idea to tell the truth.

21 **Playing policeman** – help peers to understand that when a pupil with SLCN is 'reporting on others' (telling tales), sticking to rules too rigorously or telling others to obey rules, this is something he or she has difficulty with, and their support is needed to help him or her sort out what is socially acceptable and what is not.

22 Provide opportunities to **share, negotiate and problem-solve** e.g. 'Can I share the shapes with you, please?', 'I'll start, then it's your turn,' 'Oh dear, the glue has run out – what shall we do?'

23 **My space** – during carpet times some pupils become anxious if they feel 'hemmed in' others find it difficult to sit in one place. Provide them with a carpet square or large beanbag cushion. Discuss why it is important to give each other space and to stay in the same place.

24 **Jobs** – provide the pupil with a regular, important job to do to help increase his or her feeling of worth. Choose one that is not open-ended, nor reliant on peer relationships to start with, gradually building in some interaction with others.

25 Always prepare SLCN pupils for possible **changes in routine** or personnel. Use a visual timetable to indicate what has been changed or who will be different. (See 'Visual Timetables' in Attention and Listening p. 121 strategy 29)

26 **Group rules** – use cue cards and posters with photographs, pictures or symbols, to remind pupils of social communication skills rules, e.g. interrupting, taking turns, using eye contact. Begin group work by identifying appropriate social communication skills for that specific activity. For instance, good listening, waiting for a turn to speak and looking at the speaker. Adapt to include safety issues in PE and when using equipment such as glue guns, scissors etc.

27 **Safety** – provide or create posters to support pupils' understanding of safety issues, e.g. on the apparatus in PE, the computer, talking to strangers, crossing the road etc.

Targeted Strategies and Approaches

28 Set up a **Social communication skills group** to focus on the development of specific social communication skills. Ensure pupils have opportunities to generalise skills in context by setting targets which can be supported in class and at home. Use commercially available programmes such as the Talkabout Series. See Commercial Resources on p. 161.

29 **Turn-taking** – taking turns in conversation often proves difficult for pupils with social communication needs. Knowing how to do this starts with knowing how to take turns generally. Pass a ball to and fro, stack wooden bricks in turns, share out counters saying, yours, mine etc.

30 Consider **unstructured times**, i.e. break-time, lunchtime, some open-ended classroom activities, as these can cause great anxiety and depend on the pupil's ability to make relationships and fill his or her time appropriately without direction. Some pupils with SLCN would benefit if they were involved in structured activities such as helping in the classroom, especially if they were getting some practice working as a team.

Adult support may be needed for unstructured times in class or when working as part of a team, e.g. art and craft activities or fact finding sessions involving interviewing other pupils or the public. This can cause great anxiety often resulting in a display of inappropriate behaviour.

31 **This is me** – display photos of everyone in the child's setting, discuss their names, some of their characteristics, what their interests are or which class they are in. This helps pupils to use other peoples' names and start conversations with them.

32 Support pupils in developing their emotional literacy by using the appropriate words when the emotion is being experienced. Use **Feelings cue cards** to discuss feelings and emotions generally or when specific situations have occurred. Play music and discuss the feelings that are aroused. Play different instruments and make different sounds – how do these make us feel?

33 Introduce **Talk time** – the opportunity for a pupil to talk to the class or a 'listening buddy' about their favourite topics of conversation at a specified time during the day. Use this strategy to keep pupils on topic when they 'stray' during class discussions.

34 Introduce **Social stories** (Smith 2003) to help children understand situations and how to respond and behave. E.g. write a story about a situation that the child is anxious about. Write it as a positive experience where the child is coping with the elements that distress him or her. Read it with the child regularly so that they are rehearsing and visualising themselves in a non-anxious state.

35 **Playtime buddies** – consider opportunities to develop social communication skills during break times through 'buddy' systems or by setting up small group games.

36 Establish a **home–school link book** so that misunderstandings about lessons, homework, dates, school rules, peer relationships, etc can be kept to a minimum. Make sure this book records only factual information. Do not use it to comment on the pupil's behaviour or learning performance. Both home and school should record information to share.

37 **What is it like not to be me?** Share stories that reflect diversity to support an understanding of how others may think and feel in ways that may be different to us.

38 **Role play** – use role play to practise putting oneself in another's place, act out scenes from stories (see strategy 37 above), use dressing up clothes to get into role and behave as someone else.

39 **What's the difference?** Discuss how communication changes according to where you are and who you are talking to. Practise, through role play, the different language styles or behaviour required for a range of settings, e.g. church, library, restaurant, supermarket etc.

40 **Greetings** – greeting others and instigating conversation are important social skills that help children to make friends and become part of a group. Model specific phrases to do with saying hello, joining in, sharing etc, e.g. 'Can I join in?', 'Can I play please?', 'Can I share the cars with you?'

Provide visual support – use cue cards with appropriate pictures and phrases.

41 **Conversation skills** – maintaining a conversation can be tricky. Discuss what makes a good conversation with the group. Talk about body language, taking turns, asking and answering questions, making relevant comments, how to instigate a conversation and how to end it. Make a group poster with the key points in words and pictures for reference and discussion. Make comic strip conversations for display and role play.

Commercial Resources from Language for Learning

- Feelings Pictures and Boards – Language for Learning
- Group Work Poster – Language for Learning
- Active Listening Cue Cards – Language for Learning
- Seeking Clarification Cue Cards – Language for Learning
- Feelings and Emotions – Smart Kids
- Talkabout Board Game – Speechmark
- Talkabout for Children – Speechmark
- Talkabout Self Awareness Cards – Speechmark
- Talkabout Group Cohesion Cards – Speechmark
- Moving On Up – Speechmark
- Six Social Skills Board Games – Smart Kids
- Speaking and Listening Set – Yellow Door
- Talk About How We Feel – Yellow Door
- Magnetic Behave-O-Meter and Talk Dials – Smartkids
- Developing Baseline Communication Skills – Speechmark
- The Selective Mutism Resource Manual – Speechmark
- Favourite Idioms – Speechmark

Recommended Commercial Resources from Other Sources

- Consequences Discussion Cards – Speechmark
- Reading Between the Lines – Speechmark
- Red Herrings and White Elephants – John Blake Publishing
- Saying One Thing Meaning Another – Taskmaster
- The Positive Play Programme – LDA
- Range of Pragmatic Resources – Black Sheep Press
- What Did You Say? What Do You Mean? – Jessica Kingsley Publishers
- Writing and Developing Social Stories – Speechmark

Using Strategies at Home: Social Skills Prompting

STRATEGY	PARENTS	PUPIL	COMMENTS Make notes to improve/adapt the strategy – discuss with the SENCO or TA
Social Skills Prompting There are a number of skills used in social situations that help with communication and developing good relationships with other people. Some pupils find these skills very difficult to learn. Social Communication Skills Groups are often set up in schools to systematically teach pupils these skills. Pupils need to practise regularly and in as many different situations as possible.	The SENCO in your school will tell you what is being taught in your child's social skills group. Use the same picture/symbol cards and words that are being used in school. Discuss the situation that your child is going into, reminding him/her of what he/she should say/do. Remember that the rule should be for life so teach what is acceptable in most situations, (e.g. say 'excuse me' rather than tap someone etc.	Practise what you have been doing in your social skills group at school. Let your family help by working out some 'secret' codes. Discuss how you did afterwards. Ask your parents which of their/your friends and family are good people to copy.	

Memory Skills

Observed Behaviours:

A child may be observed:

- Forgetting instructions easily
- Struggling to follow long and complex instructions despite appearing to listen
- Forgetting stages within an activity
- Forgetting equipment
- Responding to just the beginning or the end of an instruction
- Following instructions, a child may be unable to repeat or recall what needs to be done in the correct order
- Getting lost within an activity or when giving information
- Losing track in a conversation or a discussion. A child may appear to repeat themselves frequently
- Needing a longer time to process language
- Jumping to the wrong conclusions or giving a tangential reply based on only part of the information given
- Being non-compliant
- Becoming easily confused, particularly during fast conversations or discussions
- Lacking organisational skills

Positive Communication

1 **Simplify language** and speak slowly.

2 **Be relevant** – introduce new words gradually that relate to familiar situations or make links with previous experience or knowledge. Keep visual displays relevant to what is being taught so that pupils are confident to refer to them during lessons and when using objects/illustrations make sure to touch/hold up the one you are talking about.

3   Avoid or **explain non-literal language**.

4   Use **gesture and mime** to support verbal language.

5   Understanding is closely linked to the ability to remember. Give pupils time to process what has been said by using the **Ten-second rule** – once you have given an instruction allow up to 10 seconds for a response. During this time, consider the instruction: were there too many words? Was the vocabulary too difficult to understand? If the pupil does not respond after 10 seconds, either rephrase the instruction or if the right level of language was used the first time, simply repeat the instruction again.

6   Demonstrate the use of **sequential markers** as you speak by using your fingers to support the stages of an instruction, e.g. Hold your thumb when saying 'First of all …', then your index finger when you say 'then,' 'secondly' or 'next' etc. Make sure all pupils can see your hand.

7   **Emotion** – we are more likely to remember anything that is emotional, unusual, dramatic or in context. The more pupils are engaged in what they are doing the more it will be remembered, e.g. field trips, museum visits, role play, making things etc.

Universal Strategies and Approaches

8   **Regulate input** – we tend to remember best what we learn at the beginning and end of a lesson. Maximise on this by creating breaks which provide several beginnings and several endings. Repeat the main teaching points at these times.

9   **Repetition** – encourage instant recall by asking pupils to repeat exactly what you have said. Gradually build in longer and longer time delays.

10 Build in **revising and recalling** with fun activities such as word definition games, word searches, crosswords or group cartoon drawings related to the topic.

11 **Word definition activities** – help pupils to remember words by storing them efficiently. Work on word association – The Understanding the Meaning of Words strategy section has a range of word definition, sorting and classifying activities to choose from (p. 130–142).

12 **External memories** – support pupils by teaching techniques that aid memory and encourage them to take responsibility for using external memories such as, lists, drawing pictures of key points, learning mnemonics, drawing mind maps etc.

13 Encourage pupils to **revise** key points by:

1 Saying them out loud as you are more likely to remember what you have heard with your own voice.

2 Saying them out loud, then whispering them, then 'thinking' them.

3 Counting on fingers

4 Visualising what has to be done

14 **Sequence instructions** – give instructions in the same order as the action required, e.g. 'It's PE then break time' rather than, 'Before break time it's PE.'

15 **Rhymes** – remember that repetition and practise is vital to memory. Teach rhymes that help pupils remember basic concepts such as how many days there are in a month – 'Thirty days hath September …' etc.

16 **Rhythm and music** are very powerful memory aids. They support the transfer of information into long-term memory and the ability to recall it. Transfer the key points from any topic into a rhyme or a rap, add a few actions and make it fun for a winning memory jogger formula.

17 Use **mind maps** as these present a wealth of information in a memorable format, particularly if pupils are visual learners. Provide wall size mind maps of the current class topic to act as a reminder of key points covered so far.

18 Use **mnemonics** for anything that is sequenced or contains a set number of features, for example, the colours of the rainbow by initial sound – **R**ichard of **Y**ork gave battle **in vain**. Make sure that there is a long-term need for the facts to be remembered and if possible choose a mnemonic that pupils can relate to and understand.

19 **Colour code and highlight** so that key points stand out.

20 Provide **mini white boards** to reduce memory load by providing individual white boards and pens so that key points/answers can be recorded before moving on to process something else.

21 **Multiple-choice** gives pupils a limited number of alternative answers – useful for those who easily forget what they have been asked. Use when asking pupils what they would like to do, e.g. 'Do you want to use clay or paint?' or to answer a factual question, e.g. 'Is it called a duck or a swan?' Be careful though as it is common for children to say the last alternative heard.

22 Support pupils' ability to remember instructions by using **task management boards** which provide pictorial and or written support of the stages within a single activity. (See Attention and Listening, strategy 32 p. 121)

23 Provide **visual timetables** that also incorporate what has to be remembered at home such as swimming things, library books etc. (See Attention and Listening, strategy 29 p. 121)

24 **Displays** – build up visual information gradually, constructing a display to use as reference throughout the project, recapping at the start of each session.

Targeted Strategies and Approaches

25 **Messengers** – give pupils a verbal message to give to another member of the class. The message should require an answer so that it is clear that the instruction was delivered correctly and the reply remembered. Extend by delivering the message to an adult in another part of the school.

26 Play **Kim's game** – Arrange pictures representing key components of current topic work on the table. Some pictures are removed, whilst pupils look away, they then say what is missing.

27 Play versions of **'I went to market and I bought ...'** using current topic vocabulary represented by real objects or pictures and a situation. For example, pupils can be Roman soldiers preparing for battle. First pupil: 'I need a shield.' Second pupil: 'I need a shield and a helmet' etc. To extend demands on memory add more elements to the sentence, e.g. add colour, texture, size etc.

28 Provide opportunities for pupils to **practice sequences** so that memory is improved, e.g. line dancing – rehearsal increases the ability to remember longer and longer dance sequences.

29 **Memory stories** – a story will help turn an otherwise unconnected list of things into something that is interesting and therefore more memorable. For e.g. remembering what has to be brought from home the next day – letter, library book, money for trip. Tell pupils a simple story linking the items together. Encourage pupils to do this for themselves as a strategy for life.

30 Provide **personal prompt cards** with details such as address, date of birth, days of the week, numbers and spelling of numbers etc.

Recommended Commercial Resources from Other Sources

- 6 Memory Skills Board Games – Smartkids
- Memory Trainer Set – Taskmaster
- Memory Skills Fun Deck – Taskmaster
- Serial Recall Fun Deck – Taskmaster
- Auditory Memory Inferences Fun Deck – Taskmaster
- Auditory Memory for Short Stories Fun Deck – Taskmaster
- Different-Oh! – Taskmaster
- Auditory Memory for Details in Sentences Fun Deck – Taskmaster
- Sound Cubes – LDA
- Short-Term Memory Difficulties in Children – Speechmark
- Auditory Memory – Black Sheep Press

Speech

Observed Behaviours:

- Experiencing difficulties making themselves understood, they may be unintelligible
- Saying multi-syllabic or complex words inaccurately
- Simplifying words
- Experiencing difficulties with intelligibility within connected speech
- Being dysfluent, i.e. may stammer

Positive Communication

1 **Do not pretend** to understand pupils if they are unintelligible. They usually know, and this makes them feel that what they have to say is not important. Rather, ask for a repetition, using different words; this way the pupils know they are worth communicating with.

2 **Confirm** that you have understood what has been said by repeating some of the information they are giving you, for example, 'the dentist on Tuesday', etc. This relaxes pupils and gives them confidence to continue.

3 **Model** – make sure that pupils can see how you speak. Face the child, encouraging him or her to look at your mouth then speak slowly and clearly.

4 **Correcting** – try not to ask pupils to repeat sounds back to you 'correctly'. This will have little long-term effect. For example, if as an adult, you were asked to repeat the word 'loch' with a Scottish accent, you would have little difficulty; however, if asked to pronounce the same 'ch' sound in other words every time the 'ck' sound occurred, it would be very difficult.

5 **Transferring skills** – do not expect pupils with speech difficulties to be able to produce a sound spontaneously that they have been taught in isolation. For example a child who had just been taught to say the sound 'k' went to her speech and language therapy session and said, 'I touldn't tay t before told I but I tan now – listen k.'

Targeted Strategies and Approaches

6 Where possible **liaise with the speech and language therapist** if a pupil in your class accesses speech and language therapy. There will be a programme of work that can be supported and reinforced in school.

7 **Sound work** – try not to single out pupils with articulation problems to practise sounds. This is unhelpful and can hinder progress. 'Sound' work is better done in small groups with advice from your speech and language therapy service.

8 For those pupils with severe speech difficulties use visual support to ensure that they can be effective when communicating. A simple **communication board** with key vocabulary (pictures and words) for specific times of the day can be used so the pupil can point to the pictures whilst talking.

9 **Background noise** – keep classroom noise to a minimum whenever possible.

10 Play **'Straw carry'** with pieces of paper and strong straws. The pupil holds the straw in his/her mouth and places the other end on a small piece of paper. Without touching the paper, he/she sucks the straw so that his/her breath draws the paper against it. He/she then tries to walk to another part of the room without dropping the paper. This can also be played as a relay race with a small group of children.

11 Play **'Straw polo'** which is similar to blow football. The pupil blows a ping-pong ball along through a straw. Races can be set up and variations such as, blowing paper boats over water, making blow paint pictures and blowing bubbles can be added.

12 Play **Sound lotto** – see Structure and Rules: Phonology, strategy 46 p. 151 – encourage pupils to copy the relevant sounds before putting the counter on the correct picture.

13 **Do and say** – verbalise sounds along with percussion instruments, e.g. bang, bang as the drum is hit, ting, ting to accompany the triangle, mack, mack as the maracas are played etc.

14 **Technology** – take advantage of computer programmes that read aloud what has been typed so that older pupils with articulation difficulties can join in with oral presentations.

Recommended Commercial Resources from Other Sources

- Sound Loaded Scenes for Articulation – Taskmaster
- Initial T Speech Sounds card deck – Taskmaster
- M is for Me - Taskmaster
- Vowel Sounds – Taskmaster
- Write Online – Cricksoft
- Writing with Symbols – Widgit

Thinking Skills

Observed Behaviours:

- Experiencing difficulties using language for complex functions, i.e. to predict, to infer and to reason
- Struggling to assimilate all of the necessary information leading to misunderstandings
- Not considering the viewpoint of others
- Lacking organisational skills

Positive Communication

1   **Keep sentences short and 'chunk' information.** Reduce the number of clauses and keep in the correct sequence, e.g. 'Frogspawn is a mass of thousands of frog's eggs. Each egg is a little ball of jelly with a tiny embryo inside. Most embryos will turn into tadpoles, then into frogs.' Rather than, 'Frogspawn is made up of thousands of single eggs, each one having a tiny black tadpole embryo surrounded in jelly.'

2   **Simplify words and sentences** or repeat using a more simplified version, e.g. 'Why was Daniel baffled by the way Sam reacted?' 'What did Sam do – What was Daniel thinking?'

3   **Questions** – develop your questioning skills so that you encourage thinking. Grade your use of question words from easy to hard – 'Who' 'What' 'When' 'Where' before 'How' and 'Why'. Use symbol cue cards representing each one for pupils who find them confusing.

4   **Finished examples** – provide pupils with a finished version so they can see what they have to achieve in order to be able to work out how to do it.

Universal Strategies and Approaches

5   **Visual support** – when introducing a new topic start with objects and pictures. Use this visual material to encourage pupils to think about and discuss the information they can find in them. Introduce the new, specific vocabulary to this discussion so that pupils begin to use it as soon as possible – support this stage by providing vocabulary cards with the word, picture and a short definition. Then encourage questioning by providing question cards to cue pupils in.

6   Provide **flow diagrams** to support sequencing skills, e.g. a tadpole growing into a frog, the stages of working out a maths problem etc.

7   **Venn diagrams** sort information into similarities and differences which help pupils to develop the skill of manipulating facts – use them as visual support and as a sorting frame for practical work.

8   Place **symbols** by instructions to help pupils decide what has to be done, e.g. an open book by the part that has to be read, 'a pen' by the part that has to be written, 'a light bulb' when the student's own ideas are required etc.

9   **Recording** – work on recording information visually, e.g. Venn diagrams, flowcharts, prioritisation pyramids, tables (pros and cons) etc. Start by using diagrams to support information gathering. The 'How to be Brilliant at Recording in History/Geography/Science' Series by Brilliant Publications offers a huge range of photocopiable writing frames that can be easily adapted to support thinking skills across the curriculum – see Commercial Resources, p. 175.

10   **Mind maps** support thinking skills in a number of ways – a range of information can be considered at one time, connections between information/ideas/concepts are made and linked to the appropriate words.

11   For older pupils provide **colour coded text** to accompany any worksheet that requires the child to read, process information and answer questions in his or her own words. Simply highlight the question and the part of the text that contains the answer to that question with the same colour highlighter pen.

12 **Notes spaces** – for older pupils provide worksheets with note-taking boxes. Each box represents an area within the topic and contains questions prompting pupils to record relevant information. Pupils can draw pictures or write single words/short sentences.

13 Provide a range of **sorting and classifying** exercises – encouraging pupils to sort information in a variety of different ways. This supports a higher level of understanding.

14 Spend time working on **'cause and effect'** and 'prediction'. Start with personal experiences before moving on to current topic work. Role play works well for this.

15 With a group of pupils sitting in a circle take it in turns to practice **why – because** sentences. Have a series of action pictures such as a dog wagging his tail, a boy running etc. Ask 'Why is the boy running?' Stress that the answer should begin with 'Because …'. Extend this to include scenarios to do with the curriculum, e.g. 'Why did the Egyptians live near the Nile?'

16 **Expressing opinions** – work on key phrases to help express opinions, e.g.

> I like … because …
>
> I don't like … because …
>
> I think … but on the other hand …

17 **Problem solving** – create opportunities in the classroom to encourage pupils to identify a challenge or problem, suggest a solution, discuss the pros and cons and compare the solutions offered. E.g. Mrs Fellows is ill so there will be no guitar lesson for a group of six children today. All the other pupils are involved in other group activities. Ask the class to resolve what happens; to define the problem and then in pairs or small groups work out a solution. Present each solution to the class asking – What are the good things about your solution? Are there any bad things about your solution? What will be the outcome? Which is the best solution and why?

18 Teach **visualising** skills. Ask pupils to imagine something they do every day, e.g. going through their front door, walking into the hall and up the stairs then into their bedroom. Ask them to think about the pictures they 'see'. Practise doing this with information related to a particular topic –

can they 'see' people queuing for food with their ration books for example. Ask them to describe what clothes people are wearing, what sort of shop it is, what the weather is like etc.

Commercial Resources from Language for Learning

- Language for Thinking – Speechmark
- 7 Questioning Board Games – Smartkids
- Reading Between the Lines – Speechmark

Recommended Commercial Resources from Other Sources

- How to Teach Thinking and Learning for the Whole School – Sage
- Consequences Discussion Cards – Speechmark
- Learning Skills for the Whole School – Sage
- Critical Thinking Quick Take Along – Taskmaster
- Auditory Processing of WH Words – Taskmaster
- Snapshots Critical Thinking – Smart Kids
- Mind Maps for Kids – Thorsons
- Connectors Books – The Big Mistake, Nick Nelly and Jake, Uncle Al Goes to Camp – Smartkids
- How to Sparkle at Prediction Skills – Brilliant Publications
- How to be Brilliant at Recording in History – Brilliant Publications
- How to be Brilliant at Recording in Geography – Brilliant Publications
- How to be Brilliant at Recording in Science – Brilliant Publications
- Thinking Skills – Hinton House

Glossary

Terminology and jargon can be confusing and can easily lead to a breakdown in communication amongst professionals and parents. This glossary lists a range of terms linked to language skills, SLCN and school-based support that may be found within specialist reports.

Articulation	Control of speech organs in order to produce speech sounds.
Articulatory/verbal dyspraxia	A motor-programming disorder, which involves difficulties in programming the sequence of movements required to produce continuous speech.
Asperger's syndrome	An autistic spectrum disorder first described by Hans Asperger, characterised by social interaction difficulties, all absorbing narrow interests, motor clumsiness and the need for routine.
Attention control	The ability to maintain focus.
Attention deficit (hyperactivity) disorder	A disorder affecting attention control where the child is easily distracted. Hyperactivity is where the child shows high levels of restlessness as well.
Auditory discrimination	The ability to distinguish between different sounds.
Auditory memory	The ability to remember information that is heard.
Auditory working memory	The ability to remember and process information that is heard.
Autistic spectrum disorder (ASD)	Children with an autistic spectrum disorder experience impairments of social interaction, social communication and flexibility of thought. An autistic spectrum condition is a lifelong developmental disability.

Cleft lip	A split in the upper lip, which occurs during foetal development, usually associated with cleft palate.
Cleft palate	A structural abnormality whereby the roof of the mouth is not formed properly, causing problems with eating, breathing, articulation and hearing. Often occurs with a cleft lip.
Conductive hearing loss	A hearing impairment caused by a difficulty in transmitting sound through the outer or middle ear.
Delayed language development	Language development follows the typical sequence and pattern but at a slower rate.
Disordered language development	Language development does not follow the typical pattern, giving rise to language problems in one or more specific areas of language.
Dysarthria	A difficulty caused by damage to the central nervous system (neurological), which results in loss of muscle control for speech.
Dysfluency	A difficulty in producing smooth, fluent speech. This term includes stammering (UK)/stuttering (USA).
Echolalia	The repetition of words or phrases heard without understanding. Echolalia can be delayed or immediate.
Expressive language	The use of spoken language to convey a message.
Fluctuating hearing loss	Caused when children suffer from repeated colds or catarrhal infections, often undetected as the child is 'clear' at the time of a hearing check, but can have a significant effect on language development.
Global development delay	The child experiences a delay in all areas of development.
Glue ear	See 'Otitis media'.
Inclusion Development Programme (IDP)	Part of the government's strategy to support children and young people with special educational needs. Provides support for leadership teams in schools and settings and professional development materials for

school staff. Eight units for SLCN are available online.

Intonation	The rising and falling pitch patterns of language that express a wide range of meaning.
Mnemonic	An aid to memory, e.g. initial letters of a sentence to spell a word or a picture accompanying a word.
Morphology	The way in which word structures change to signal a change in meaning, e.g. sleep, sleeping, slept, asleep.
Otitis media	The most common form of conductive hearing loss, caused by catarrhal infections spreading to the middle ear via the Eustachian tube. Often referred to as 'glue ear'.
Phoneme	The individual sounds we use when pronouncing sounds. There are approximately forty in the English language.
Phonological awareness	The ability to think consciously about speech sounds and to use these skills within literacy.
Phonological delay	Phonological development follows a typical pattern, but at a slower rate. Phonological processes appear to persist beyond the age at which they should disappear, e.g. reduction of clusters so 'sl' in 'sleeping' becomes 'seeping'.
Phonological disorder	Phonological development does not follow a typical pattern of development, i.e. phonological processes which do not occur during typical development are present.
Phonology	The **speech** sound system of a language – the rules which govern how sounds are organised in words in order to convey different meanings.
Pragmatics	The use of language in social situations, including conversational skills and the understanding and use of non-verbal communication.
Receptive language	Understanding spoken language.

Selective mutism or talking	A child does not to speak in certain situations, e.g. school but can speak in others e.g. home.
Semantics	The meaning of words and sentences.
Sensori-neural hearing loss	Hearing impairment as a result of damage to the inner ear or nerve pathways to the brain.
Signalong	A system of hand shapes and movements which relate to the spoken grammatical form of English and can therefore be used to illustrate what the speaker is saying.
Social communication skills	See pragmatics.
Specific language impairment (SLI)	A primary and specific, persistent receptive or expressive language disorder/impairment, in the absence of any other difficulties. It does not include children or young people who do not develop language because of intellectual or physical disability, hearing loss, emotional problems or environmental deprivation.
Specific learning difficulties	Difficulty in acquiring skills in specific areas, e.g. literacy and numeracy. Difficulties include dyslexia and dyscalculia.
Speech, language and communication framework (SLCF)	Recognised competency framework published by The Communication Trust, setting out the knowledge and skills required by those working with children and young people with SLCN.
Speech, language and communication needs (SLCN)	A wide ranging term used to encompass all speech, language and communication difficulties, i.e. difficulties communicating effectively with others; understanding and/or using language. Includes a range of complexity of needs from long-term persistent communication disabilities through to more transient language delay as a result of limited life experiences.
Stammering (stuttering)	See 'Dysfluency'.

| Syntax | The rule system which governs the structure of language at a word, phrase and sentence level. |
| Theory of mind | Awareness that others have different thoughts, feelings and knowledge from yourself. |

Syntax

References

Commissioning Support Programme (2011) *Speech, Language and Communication Needs: Introduction; Needs assessment; Whole system mapping and design; User involvement and consultation; Workforce planning; Evaluating Outcomes.* CSP.

Communication Trust, The (2013) *The Communication Commitment.* www.thecommunicationtrust.org.uk/projects/communication-commitment/

DCSF (2008) *The Bercow Report: A review of services for children and young people (0–19) with speech, language and communication needs.* Nottingham, DCSF.

DCSF (2008) *Better Communication: An action plan to improve services for children and young people with speech, language and communication needs.* Nottingham, DCSF.

DfE (2011) *Teachers' Standards: Guidance for school leaders, school staff and governing bodies.* DfE.

DfE (2013) *The National Curriculum in England: Framework document.* DfE.

DfE and DoH (2014) *Special Educational Needs and Disability Code of Practice: 0 to 25 years.* DfE & DoH.

Dockrell, J. and Lindsay, G. (2012) *Better Communication Research Programme: The relationship between speech, language and communication needs and behavioural, emotional and social difficulties.* DfE.

Dockrell, J., Bakopoulou, I., Law, J., Spencer, S. and Lindsay, G. (2012) *Better Communication Research Programme: Communication supporting classroom observation tool.* DfE.

Feinstein, L. and Duckworth, K. (2006) *Development in the Early Years: Its importance for school performance and adult outcomes.* London, Centre for Research on the Wider Benefits of Learning Institute of Education.

Gascoigne, M. (2006) *Supporting Children with Speech, Language and Communication Needs within Integrated Children's Services* RCSLT Position Paper. London, RCSLT.

Gascoigne, M. (2012) *Commissioning for Better Speech, Language and Communication Outcomes* in Gascoigne, M (ed.) (2012) *Better Communication:*

Shaping speech, language and communication services for children and young people. London, RCSLT.

Gross, J. (2011) *Two Years On: Final report of the Communication Champion for Children.* London, Office of the Communication Champion.

Gross, J. (2013) *Time to Talk.* Oxon, Routledge/NASEN.

Hayden, S. and Jordan, E. (2015) *Identification, Assessment and Intervention: A practical guide for speech and language therapists and specialist teachers working in mainstream classrooms.* Kidderminster, Language for Learning.

Hayden, S. and Jordan, E. (2012) *Language for Learning in the Secondary School: A practical guide for supporting students with speech, language and communication needs.* Oxon, Routledge.

Johnson, M. and Player, C. (2009) *Active Listening for Learning.* Stafford, QEd.

Lee, W. (2013) *A Generation Adrift: A case for speech, language and communication to take a central role in schools' policy and practice.* London, The Communication Trust.

Lindsay, G., Dockrell, J., Desforges, M., Law, J. and Peacey, N. (2010) *Meeting the Needs of Children and Young People with Speech, Language and Communication Difficulties,* International Journal of Language and Communication Disorders Vol 45.

Lindsay, G., Dockrell, J., Law, J. and Roulstone, S. (2012) *The Better Communication Research Programme: Improving provision for children and young people with speech, language and communication needs.* DfE.

Mason, V. and Milne, E. (2014) *Speech, Language and Communication Pocketbook.* Alresford, Teachers' Pocketbooks.

Ofsted (2012) *School Inspection Handbook.* Manchester, Ofsted.

Parsons, S. and Branagan, A. (2014) *Word Aware: Teaching vocabulary across the day, across the curriculum.* Milton Keynes, Speechmark.

Smith, C. (2003) *Writing and Developing Social Stories: Practical interventions in autism.* Milton Keynes, Speechmark.

Speake, J. (2003) *How to Identify and Support Children with Speech and Language Difficulties.* Wisbech, LDA.

Spooner, L. and Woodcock, J. (2010) *Teaching Children to Listen: A practical approach to developing children's listening skills.* London, Continuum.

Welton, J. (2004) *What Did You Say? What Do You Mean?* London, Jessica Kingsley Publishers.

Appendix 1: Suppliers of Commercial Resources

Supplier	Website
AMS Educational	www.amseducational.co.uk
Black Sheep Press	www.blacksheeppress.co.uk
Brilliant Publications	www.brilliantpublications.co.uk
Cricksoft	www.cricksoft.com
Dorling Kindersley	www.dk.co.uk
Featherstone Education	www.bloombury.com/uk
Galt Toys	www.galttoys.com
Hinton House	www.hintonpublishers.com
Hope Educational	www.hope-education.co.uk
Jessica Kingsley Publishers	www.jkp.com
John Blake Publishing Ltd	www.johnblakepublishing.co.uk
Language for Learning	www.languageforlearning.com
LDA Learning	www.ldalearning.com
Living and Learning	www.ldalearning.com
Orchard Toys	www.orchard-toys.org.uk
Oxford University Press	www.global.oup.com
Sage	www.uk.sagepub.com
SEMERC	www.semerc.com
Smartkids (UK) Ltd	www.smartkids.co.uk
Speechmark	www.speechmark.net
Taskmaster	www.taskmasteronline.co.uk
Teachers' Pocketbooks	www.teacherspocketbooks.co.uk

Supplier	Website
TES Connect	www.tes.co.uk
Thorsons Publishers	www.amazon.co.uk
Widgit Software	www.widgit.com
Winslow Press	www.winslowpress.com
Yellow Door	www.yellow-door.net

Appendix 2: Language for Learning® in the Primary School Training Opportunities

Language for Learning offers training courses for school staff

Informative, practical and realistic

These ideas can be easily transferred into the classroom. The course has given me ideas to use with the whole class

Half and Whole day Training Courses

Practical Workshops

Beautifully created and presented

Identification and assessment	Providing visual support

Improving social communication skills	Developing memory	Developing listening skills

Supporting vocabulary development	Providing access across the curriculum

Developed in 2000 by Sue Hayden and Emma Jordan, Language for Learning® is a joint health and education non-profit making project owned by Worcestershire County Council and Worcestershire Health and Care NHS Trust. It provides training courses and resources for practitioners and parents from Early Years to Key Stage 4 and training materials for trainers to deliver these courses within their own authorities.

Language for Learning, Speech and Language Centre,
Franche Clinic, Marlpool Place, Kidderminster,
Worcestershire, DY11 5BB
Tel: 01562 752749

www.languageforlearning.co.uk
@LforLearning

Index